BOOKS, BLACKBOARDS, AND BULLETS

School Shootings and Violence in America

Marcel Lebrun

Rowman & Littlefield Education
Lanham • New York • Toronto • Plymouth, UK

Published in the United States of America
by Rowman & Littlefield Education
A Division of Rowman & Littlefield Publishers, Inc.
A wholly owned subsidary of The Rowman & Littlefield Publishing
Group, Inc.
4501 Forbes Boulevard, Suite 200, Lanham, Maryland 20706
www.rowmaneducation.com

Estover Road
Plymouth PL6 7PY
United Kingdom

British Library Cataloguing in Publication Information Available

Library of Congress Cataloging-in-Publication Data

Lebrun, Marcel, 1957–
  Books, blackboards, and bullets : school shootings and violence in
America / Marcel Lebrun.
      p. cm.
  Includes bibliographical references.
  ISBN-13: 978-1-57886-866-7 (cloth : alk. paper)
  ISBN-10: 1-57886-866-1 (cloth : alk. paper)
  ISBN-13: 978-1-57886-904-6 (electronic)
  ISBN-10: 1-57886-904-8 (electronic)
  1. School shootings—United States. 2. School violence—United States.
3. School violence—United States—Prevention. I. Title.
  LB3013.32.L43 2009
  371.7'820973—dc22   2008021920

∞™ The paper used in this publication meets the minimum requirements
of American National Standard for Information Sciences—Permanence of
Paper for Printed Library Materials, ANSI/NISO Z39.48-1992.
Manufactured in the United States of America.

This book is dedicated to all the victims of school violence. It is written for all the lives that have been cut short due to violence and the loss of all that could have been created.

I would like to thank my family, friends, and my colleagues at Plymouth State University for all their professional and personal support.

I would like to thank my graduate assistant Megan Brown for all her assistance in doing the research and typing some of the information.

Contents

Preface

School violence is a multifaceted, multilayered, complex problem that has manifested itself in our present school system. The school system was developed to educate the future generations of this country and its mission was and still is to create responsible, caring, committed, and patriotic citizens who are able to function harmoniously within a community. It was supposed that all citizens would graduate from this system and become contributing members to the betterment of all.

Our schools have become warehouses for children with insurmountable social, economic, physical, and psychological issues. The present school system as it exists, the teacher preparation programs at universities, the funding of education, and the lack of community resources all contribute to the challenges that influence the development of violence in the schools. The schools in many communities have poor physical features, are rundown, and are oftentimes substandard, thus leading to the lack of pride and loyalty toward the institution. Does creating a sense of loyalty and pride prevent school violence? Many people agree that if you are connected and have a sense of belonging to a place or person you are less likely to destroy or damage it.

Many statistics for violence do not match the norms for American society. The U.S. Department of Justice has researched and kept accurate data on crime rates for many years. Overall crime rates have decreased; yet, every time there is a school shooting, the press will magnify it to show that school violence is an out-of-control phenomenon. Educators have long stated that violence has increased because schools are not safe, that teachers do not know or are not trained how to handle students with multiple issues and are often using outdated, ineffective methodology to deal with violence. Within this ineffectiveness, educators are compounding and sustaining the violence.

It is my belief that better-trained teachers who receive crisis-intervention techniques are more likely to be proactive rather than reactive when dealing with confrontational students. Better-organized schools are more likely to become environments that are safe, respectful of student diversity, and welcoming. School violence, shootings, stabbings, and assaults can happen anywhere or anytime. It would be foolish to assume that a certain town, city, or school is immune to this issue. It can happen to anyone. Educators and students agree that school violence and school safety cohabit together because our society has allowed our schools to become unsafe due to the increase in dysfunction in both families and communities. Violence can deprive all who encounter it of a safe and productive learning environment.

Schools have tried to take extra precautions to keep students safe. Many schools have tried and succeeded in keeping weapons out of the classrooms. They have utilized a variety of means, such as metal detectors, locker searches, bag checks, locked exit doors, and increased adult supervision and have started to win the battle toward making a school safer. However, it is sad to state that weapons do still get into the school, shootings do occur, and students are hurt and/or killed.

Do we have to make our schools into armed prisons to keep the students and staff safe? Taking action can and will save lives, prevent injury, and minimize property damage in the moments of crisis. It is up to the educators to make sure that all schools have a crisis plan in place, and if one is not present, to begin developing it. It is my belief that all must be aware. All must be responsible. It is no longer a case of passing the responsibility to police or emergency responders. All faculties and staff must provide input and feedback about what can be done during a crisis.

Conversations must begin on the part of all facets of the educational system. Each individual community must assess their major and minor problems and understand the connection to and link with student violence and crime. The days of playing ostrich are over. Each individual community or school must assess the environment and figure out a plan of action on how to address these problems in a proactive way.

Educators must be vigilant and on alert. Schools are places of learning; however, they are very vulnerable places. Educators must assess their vulnerability and plan accordingly. Good planning, good discussions, feedback, and awareness will most often facilitate a rapid and coordinated effective response. Anything less than this will result in the loss of young lives and the destruction of safe zones for children, and will impact how society views education. The time for action is now.

1

Looking at the Problem of School Violence

Schools are a reflection of the society they are in. How does one evaluate American society today? Is it a place of freedom, compassion, peace, and friendliness, or a place of competition, fear, anger, aggression, and lack of respect? Are children in this day and age brought up to be safe, responsible, and respectful citizens? Many would argue that the decline of the school system is symptomatic of the decline of the family values, the lack of good role modeling, and the lack of direction on the part of adults.

Children learn and follow by example. Who are the role models today? Britney Spears, who appears all over the media engaged in self-destructive behavior! Madonna and many rock groups, as well as some gangster rappers! George W. Bush! CEOs of the largest companies! Or should they be the child's family, friends, and local school?

Our schools should be a safe haven for teaching and learning, free of crime and violence. Even though statistics have shown that a student is safer at school than away from it, any instance of crime or violence at school not only affects the individuals involved but also may disrupt the educational process and affect bystanders, the school itself, and the surrounding community (Henry, 2000).

For all in the schools, victimization at school can have lasting effects. In addition to experiencing loneliness, depression, and adjustment difficulties (Crick & Bigbee, 1998; Crick & Grotpeter, 1996; Nansel et al., 2001; Prinstein, Boergers, & Vemberg, 2001; Storch et al., 2003), victimized children are more prone to truancy (Ringwalt, Ennett, & Johnson, 2003), poor academic performance (Wei & Williams, 2004), dropping out of school (Beauvais et al., 1996), and violent behaviors (Nansel et al., 2003). Due to increased violence more educators have decided that it is not worth it to fight the battle and have left the profession to pursue less dangerous employment.

Violence does not suddenly appear in a school environment or community; rather, it grows like a cancer. It begins small and benign and slowly takes over the whole organism, till finally it consumes all that is living and good. Has our society becomes so permissive that there are no longer any constraints and limits, no one saying, "No," allowing all to revert back to one's id and basic instincts?

Violence enters human lives because it is a way that many individuals have learned to meet their needs and wants: "It is only by using a gun or other weapon that people will give me what I want, and if they won't, I will take it by force." This society and many like it throughout the world have been divided into several compartments: the ones who have it, those who don't and want it, those who have no chance in hell of ever getting it, and those who are born to never get anything. By creating the haves and have-nots we have said to the have-nots that they should be satisfied with their draw in life and not want more.

The following social issues of poverty, mental illness, lack of education, and lack of support and resources for all have contributed to the increase in violence both in society and in schools. The Centers for Disease Control and Prevention have issued several reports since 1997 stating that the United States has the highest rates of childhood homicide, suicide, and firearms-related deaths of any of the world's twenty-six wealthiest nations. Nearly 75 percent of murders of children in the industrialized world occur in this country.

Subsequent reports have found that younger and younger children are becoming perpetrators as well as victims. Juvenile crime in the United States is increasing at a much faster rate than adult crime.

Youth violence is widespread in the United States. It is the second leading cause of death for young people between the ages of ten and twenty-four: 5,570 young people aged ten to twenty-four were murdered—an average of sixteen each day—in 2003 (CDC, 2007). Over 780,000 violence-related injuries in young people aged ten to twenty-four were treated in U.S. emergency rooms in 2004 (CDC, 2007). In a 2005 nationwide survey, 36 percent of high school students reported being in a physical fight during the past twelve months (CDC, 2007). Nearly 7 percent of high school students in 2005 reported taking a gun, knife, or club to school in the thirty days before the survey (CDC, 2007). An estimated 30 percent of kids between sixth and tenth grade report being involved in bullying (CDC, 2007).

Youth violence can be defined and described in several ways. It can begin in early childhood and continue into early adulthood. It can include anything from slapping to armed robbery and everything in between. Children and adolescents can manifest these behaviors in acts of rage, bullying, or even physical attacks upon other children. Oftentimes adults are very aware of the physical harm that is caused by these children.

The physical attacks show specific traces of violence and seem easier to prove and have led to children being hurt, traumatized, and requiring hospital care or even being shot or killed. The emotional harm that violent children inflict upon other children is much more difficult to prove and seems to have more powerful long-term effects and creates more emotional instability on the part of the victim. It seems that the victim is tortured mentally and emotionally without ever receiving any type of physical attack or injury.

Many factors make juveniles more likely to commit and to become victims of crimes. One major factor is drug use. In economically deprived areas, young people are recruited to make fast money, which is quick and dirty, and these juveniles are less likely to be punished by the legal system than an adult dealer. One just needs to look at the fast money that can be made on the streets by these juveniles.

They can make a whole bundle of cash in an afternoon as compared to working at McDonald's for eight hours and have $60 dollars to show for their efforts. The draw of the fast life and fast cash is too intoxicating for these kids and therefore they are drawn to the negative underworld of the streets. It is a place that has no safe return. They either become users themselves or are killed in some drug deal that goes wrong.

The second reason given for the rise in youth violence is the availability of illegal guns, which are widely accessible in some communities. Guns often accompany the drug trade, and guns in the community create a climate of fear for all residents. Where there are guns there are gangs. The National Youth Gang Center reported large numbers of gangs and members, over half concentrated in three states, California being number one, followed by Illinois and Texas. The center stated that "No state is gang-free. There are youth gangs emerging in new localities, especially smaller and rural locations" (McCarthy, 1998).

What underlies the youth violence epidemic? Juvenile participation in drug trade, gangs, economic social factors, and personal emotional factors all contribute to the likeliness that violence will enter the lives of children and adolescents. Hawkins, Lishner, and Catalano's (1995) risk and resiliency theory identifies risk factors for youth violence at four different levels or domains.

Risk Factors

Neighborhood Level

Availability of guns; community laws, or norms favorable to drug use, guns, and crime; and media portrayals of violence, low neighborhood attachment, community disorganization, and extreme economic deprivation.

Family Level

Poor family management practices, absence of clear expectations and standards of behaviors, excessively severe or inconsistent punishment, parental failure to monitor children, family conflict, favorable parental attitudes and involvement in violent behavior, physical abuse, sexual abuse, and/or neglect by parents.

School Level

Persistent or early onset of antisocial behavior, persistent or early academic failure, lack of commitment to school, and association with peers who engage in violent or problem behaviors.

Individual-Peer Level

Alienation and rebelliousness, lack of impulse control, sensation seeking, constitutional factors such as heredity, and the role of addictions (Hawkins, Lishner, & Catalano, 1995). At the individual level one must examine the biological and personal history factors that increase the risk of being a perpetrator or a victim. A history of personality disorders and behaving aggressively or experiencing abuse makes it more likely that the child will resort to violence as a way of coping.

Societal Level

One must investigate the societal factors such as social norms that create a climate in which violence is encouraged or inhibited. When investigating factors around violence the following must be taken into account: health, economic, educational, and social policies that maintain economic or social inequalities between groups in society.

Often violence is considered a problem of adolescence, but the statistics are showing earlier acting-out behaviors on the part of young children. Some children are manifesting early violence shortly after birth. The increasing rates of child abuse, child neglect, and child victimization are creating a generation of children who have no sense of belonging and commitment to the adults in their lives. The cycle of hate, violence, and unstable mental health continues.

School violence and the issues surrounding this phenomenon seem to have developed a language of their own. The increase in legality and more arrests and court appearances have warranted a series of definitions of selected violent and disruptive incidents. The Office of the New York State Education Department in their 2005 Reporting of Violent and Disruptive Incidents by Public Schools Report developed the following guidelines in defining specific violent behaviors. The committee defined the following terms to make it easier for law enforcers to be specific around youth violence and how it was manifested. The language defined below is easily interpreted and provides concrete guidelines.

Assault with serious physical injury is defined as intentionally or recklessly causing serious physical injury to another person with or without a weapon. As a rule the injury requires hospitalization—usually it is a bullet wound, stab wound, broken bones, cuts, concussions, or any other injury involving risk of death or disfigurement.

Assault with physical injury is defined as intentionally or recklessly causing physical injury to another person with or without a weapon. This is usually a minor injury not requiring hospitalization and is usually treated by a school nurse.

Reckless endangerment is defined a subjecting individuals to danger by recklessly engaging in conduct that creates a substantial risk of physical injury, but no actual physical injury.

Criminal harassment means striking, shoving, or kicking another person or subjecting another person to unwanted physical contact with the intent to harass, annoy, or alarm another person. As a general rule, this is the category that applies when a student strikes another student without intending to injure that student. It would cover horseplay and similar conduct.

Intimidation, harassment, menacing, or *bullying* are defined as threatening, stalking, or seeking to coerce or compel a person to do something; engaging in verbal or physical conduct that threatens another with harm, including intimidation through the use of epithets or slurs involving race, ethnicity, national origin, religion, religious practices, gender, sexual orientation, age, or disability that substantially disrupts the educational process. This category does not involve physical contact but does involve the threat of harm.

Criminal mischief is intentional or reckless damaging of the property of the school or of another person, including, but not limited to, vandalism and the defacing of property with graffiti.

A total of seventeen different types of violent and disruptive behavior have been tracked by state agencies and schools nationwide (Office of the State Comptroller State Education Report, n.d.). All incidents must be reported by the schools, and each must be reported to the state agency. All seventeen types of violent and disruptive behavior are considered serious, but some are considered more serious than others in their impact on school climate and school safety. The seventeen different types of reportable incidents are:

1. Homicide;
2. Sexual offense;

3. Kidnapping;
4. Assault with serious physical injury;
5. Assault with physical injury;
6. Arson;
7. Robbery;
8. Reckless endangerment;
9. Criminal harassment;
10. Intimidation, harassment, menacing, or bullying;
11. Burglary, larceny, or other theft offenses;
12. Criminal mischief;
13. Bomb threat;
14. False alarm;
15. Other disruptive incidents;
16. Possession, but not use, of a weapon; and
17. Use, sale, or possession of drugs or alcohol.

National statistics are collected and used to form trends and analysis of school violence throughout the states. This data is then correlated to other factors and issues and a yearly report is presented to the U.S. Justice Department.

Each year, 1.6 million people worldwide lose their lives to violence. It is the leading cause of death for people aged fifteen to forty-four years. Violence places a massive burden on national economies. Costs in health care, law enforcement, and lost productivity are in the billions. Violence will not be solved by a single group. It will be a collaborative effort involving a wide range of professional expertise, including medicine, psychology, sociology, criminology, education, and economics.

So what do we need to do? Does America need a complete overhaul of its systems, values, and beliefs to become a less violent society? Or are we headed for a continued series of school shootings, mall mass murders, serial killings, and their devastation? Can America become a kinder and more accepting place? Is it too late? We were once cavemen; are we headed back to a time of kill or be killed?

Change must begin at the grassroots level, where families teach children the difference between right and wrong, schools teach children to become better citizens, and society values individuals who have the skills and values to be effective participants in a collective society. This society creates a system where all individuals have the ability to be successful and happy.

It is with a sense of compassion and caring that we can make a change. We all must accept responsibility for all children; we need to give them the opportunity to succeed and live the American Dream. The Constitution guarantees equality for all, so when is this supposed to happen? I am waiting.

2

Statistics of School Violence Past and Present

Various government agencies have collected crime statistics for many years, and the data has indicated a variety of trends and predictors. The first area to show growth was homicide. In 2004, 5,292 young people aged ten to twenty-four were murdered—an average of fifteen each day (CDC, 2007). Fifteen young people per day—what is going on in this country?

Homicide was the second leading cause of death for young people aged ten to twenty-four years old (CDC, 2007). Among ten to twenty-four-year-olds, 85 percent (4,518) of homicide victims were male and 15 percent (774) were female (CDC, 2007). Among homicide victims aged ten to twenty-four years old, 81 percent were killed with a firearm (CDC, 2007). Among ten to twenty-four-year-olds, homicide is the leading cause of death for African Americans, the second leading cause of death for Hispanics, and the third leading cause of death for American Indians, Alaska Natives, and Asian/Pacific Islanders (CDC, 2007).

Homicide rates among non-Hispanic, African American males ten to twenty-four years old (53.1 per 100,000) exceed those of Hispanic males (20.1 per 100,000) and non-Hispanic white males in the same age group (3.3 per 100,000) (CDC,

2007). Homicide, the act of killing another human being! What possesses a child or young person to choose this type of final aggression? What is going on in this child's or youth's mind at the time they pull the trigger, stab, or beat another human being to death? It would be wonderful if we could read the mind of this individual to really understand the motivation to kill. Or is it a reaction to a momentum that has no way of ending but in a death?

Young people using violence do not suddenly pick up a gun or knife one day and kill. Rather, it is a series of actions and life events that propels a young person to kill. The factors that may influence are many. How does the combination of these factors come together to create a monster? One must also ask whether a young person is really a monster or just a victim of circumstances. Was he born to pull a trigger? He had no chance right from the beginning. His destiny was to be exactly what he became—a killer, an individual who begins life troubled and continues through childhood troubled only to find trouble when he is old enough to obtain the weapon of choice. Is he really to blame for doing the act, or is society responsible for developing and fostering his development into one of society's rejects?

In 2005, more than 721,000 young people aged ten to twenty-four were treated in emergency departments for injuries sustained from violence (CDC, 2007). In 2005, of a nationally representative sample of students in grades nine to twelve, 3.6 percent reported being in a physical fight one or more times in the previous twelve months that resulted in injuries that had to be treated by a doctor or nurse (CDC, 2006b).

In a 2005 nationally representative sample of youth in grades nine through twelve (CDC, 2006b), 35.9 percent reported being in a physical fight in the twelve months preceding the survey; the prevalence was higher among males (43.4 percent) than females (28.1 percent). Youth are taken to hospitals daily due to violence. Is there a belief on the part of the youth that it is okay to fight because she will get better; the hospital and doctors will fix her?

One must look at the bigger picture and discover the true reasons why children and youth strike and hurt one another. Individuals who have learned to hit will use this coping skill to deal with problems. If they are unable to communicate what it is they want or need in a way that will get them their item or service or choice, they will take it by force.

The part of aggressor is predictable: he will take, he will hit, he will hurt, and he will walk away. The victim on the receiving end will suffer trauma, physical injury, hospitalization, and possibly recovery. What is happening in schools where children and youths are being attacked and assaulted in class and in the hallways? Where is the adult supervision? Where are the security measures to ensure safety for all? What are the social factors influencing the school climate? How proactive are school officials in preventing and planning for physical attacks within their school walls?

More students are carrying weapons to school—18.5 percent reported carrying a weapon (gun, knife, or club); 5.4 percent carried a gun on one or more days. Males were more likely than females to carry a weapon (29.8 percent versus 7.1 percent) on one or more days; males also were more likely than females to carry a gun on one or more days (9.9 percent versus 0.9 percent) (CDC, 2007).

Bringing a gun or weapon to school for what? To protect or to intimidate? Weapons have been part of this country's existence since early times. There was a belief that a weapon, no matter what, would protect against forces that lurked in the darkness. The dangers were real and anticipated: be it animals, enemies, or other perceived danger, Americans were ready to protect themselves. In these troubled times the enemy is no longer animals or conquering soldiers or native Americans; today the enemy is ourselves.

The enemy is something that grows within many minds and souls of the American population. The dangers have been created within our borders by our own behaviors. We have created unsafe schools and communities. We have created economic disparity. We have created the haves and the have-nots. The land of the free and brave is no longer free. We say we are, but we are not free from fear; we lock our doors, put security alarms everywhere, and protect our children from dangerous people. We are prisoners within our own walls.

Many Americans live in fear of being attacked on the way home from work, shopping in a mall, or just taking a walk in the park. For many, this fear has been transmitted into a belief that the only way we can be safe is to be armed. However, being armed means you can also shoot and stab someone else in the name of protecting yourself. Children see adult behaviors and beliefs and model these.

Children and youths taking weapons to school have the same level of motivation as their parents: I will protect myself at all cost. No one will hurt me because I can protect myself and hurt them first. Whether the fear of safety is real or perceived does not matter; the youth of America will be ready regardless—they will shoot first and ask questions later.

Fighting on school property also has shown a major increase from previous years. In a 2005 nationally representative sample of youth in grades nine through twelve, 13.6 percent (18.2 percent of male students and 8.8 percent of female students) reported being in a physical fight on school property in the twelve months preceding the survey.

In the twelve months preceding the survey, 29.8 percent of students reported having property stolen or deliberately damaged on school property. Six percent of students did not go to school on one or more days in the thirty days preceding the survey because they felt unsafe at school or on their way to or from school. Six-and-a-half percent reported carrying a weapon (gun, knife, or club) on school property on one or more days in the thirty days preceding the survey. And 7.9

percent reported being threatened or injured with a weapon on school property one or more times in the twelve months preceding the survey (CDC, 2006b).

Comparing the statistics from year to year, one can see that not much changes; youths still use violence to solve their problems. They are unable to understand that differences are not solved by the fist or the gun. It is still reported that students fight as a way of expressing or releasing their frustration and anger. Due to their nature, schools are locations where kids of many colors and personalities come together to share a place of learning. But what they learn early on is that school can be a nasty, unsafe place where you defend and protect yourself or you become the victim.

An estimated 30 percent of sixth to tenth graders in the United States were either bullies, targets of bullying, or both (Nansel et al., 2001). Bullying has become such a problem in this country that many people see it as a normal facet of life and growing up. It is to be expected that all children will experience some sort of bullying and will manage. There seems to be a readiness to accept bullying as part of every child's school experience.

Less than 1 percent of all homicides and suicides among school-age youth occur on school grounds, on the way to or from school, or on the way to or from school-sponsored events (Anderson et al., 2001). Bullying is a phenomenon that has existed for years and seems to be growing. In some communities it is becoming more sophisticated, more intentional, and more dangerous. Children and youths are falling victim to bullying behaviors in record numbers. Please check the full chapter on bullying in this book.

From 1992 to 1999, perpetrators of school-associated homicides were nine times as likely as victims to have exhibited some form of suicidal behavior before the event and were more than twice as likely as victims to have been bullied by their peers (Anderson et al., 2001). More than half of the incidents over this period were preceded by some signal, such as threats, notes, or journal entries that indicated the potential for the coming event (Anderson et al., 2001).

Most events occurred during the transition times around the start of the school day, the lunch period, and at the end of the school day (Anderson et al., 2001). In 2005, persons under the age of twenty-five constituted 44.5 percent of all persons arrested for violent crime and 53.9 percent of all persons arrested for property crime in the United States (FBI, 2007).

Persons under the age of twenty-five accounted for 49.6 percent of those arrested for murder and 62.0 percent of those arrested for robbery in 2005 (FBI, 2007). Students involved in these kinds of crimes are more likely to have a set of characteristics and life events that predispose them to acting out in a violent way. Future chapters will explore the varying factors that create and influence violent youths and children. The search for answers as to why children use violence is a conversation that must be ongoing and challenge the myths and perceptions that people have around the issue of school and personal violence.

3

Profile of a School Shooter

Police and educators across this country are alerting many communities what to look for when they are dealing with troubled youth. One never knows which student will resort to violence to solve his or her problems. The unpredictability of the situation or the child's behavior makes it very difficult to predict with certain accuracy that there will be a school shooting. Lists meant to screen students for the possibility of school violence are at times foolish because many students will fulfill the numerous criteria but will not have the intent.

Students who become violent become that way after a series of many factors and life events. The shooter does not wake up one morning and decide, "I am going to kill my teachers and fellow students." Violence has become a staple of American life, and children and youths are the victims of violence. Some see it in action, and many are fascinated by the violence in games, movies, and television. Thousands of children and youths live in environments riddled with crime and violence. Their only models of survival are using violence for protection and conflict resolution.

The sad part is that many youths and children do not feel safe either at school or at home. There have been increases in bullying, teacher assault, and student-to-student physical altercations. Research is showing us that bullies of today are much more violent than those of yesteryear. Violence is coming into youths' lives indirectly and directly—indirectly by the images they see on television and directly when they have to walk through drug- and gang-infested neighborhoods to get to school. The issue of violence has gotten out of hand because every school child has witnessed violence firsthand.

Many commonalities exist in the life of a potential shooter. Many are diagnosed with one of the following disorders: conduct disorder, oppositional defiant disorder, psychopathology disorders and personality disorders, and many have mental health issues. So many of these students have experienced and continue to experience violence that violence is not pathological behavior but a logical adaptation to living in a violent environment.

Many youths live with parents or other adults that are violent to each other. When parents are out of control, the child loses the rock of stability of the family structure. Oftentimes children are dragged into adult conflicts and either become part of the problem or manifest their anger and frustration toward others.

Assessment of a potential school shooter can be reviewed from many different angles. Please find below the quick assessment tool titled "ABC Profile of a School Shooter." This quick tool is meant as a guide to begin discussion around the behaviors of certain at-risk students.

ABC Profile of a School Shooter

Access to a firearm, has previously brought a weapon to school
Blames others for difficulties
Changes in behavior is dramatic
Difficulty with impulse control

Evidence of frequent disciplinary problems
Feelings of hopelessness
Gives away possessions
Homicidal tendencies
Involved in drug, alcohol, or other substance abuse dependency
Joins a gang or an antisocial group on the fringe of peer acceptance
Kills or tortures small animals
Little or no supervision and support from parents or caring adult
Mood changes and often depressed
Name calling, cursing, and/or abusive language
Often reflects anger and frustration and the dark side of life in school writing
Preoccupation with fighting, guns, and other weapons
Quiet and withdrawn at times, usually before acting out
Reading materials dealing with violent themes, rituals, and abuse
Self-destructive or has attempted suicide
Truant from school
Uncontrollable tantrums and angry outbursts
Violent threats when angry
Wetting of the bed
X-posed to secondhand violence
Younger children are usually bullied or intimidated by these individuals
Zeal for games with violent themes

The FBI has developed a Threat Assessment Protocol that can be found on its website. The model that has been developed is to assess the potential likeliness that the threat made by a student will be carried out. The FBI developed the Four-Prong Assessment Model as way to help schools and communities deal with the possibility of a crisis situation. The model helps educators, law enforcement officials, mental health practitioners, and all those who work with youths begin the discussion of whether the person making the threat has the intention, ability, and the means to act on the threat.

It is crucial that these individuals make the proper determination when they are assessing the potential risk. The model speaks about the totality of the circumstances known about the student so that an appropriate and accurate threat assessment can be made. School psychologists, counselors, specialists, teachers, and administrators are all on the front lines to assess and collect information about what is happening at the moment a student makes a threat.

It is important that in this moment an assessment reveals whether the threat is low, medium, or high and what appropriate interventions are at each level. One must also constantly be aware of what is happening in this youth's life in order to determine whether the student is capable of and under enough stressors to carry out the threat.

As implied, the FBI Four-Prong Assessment model has four parts: (1) personality of the student, (2) family dynamics, (3) school dynamics and the student's role in those dynamics, and (4) social dynamics. (FBI, 2007). This assessment is based on the totality of the circumstances. It is a way to understand all the different dynamics that will be of importance or will influence the behavior of the child or youth to act out.

One must also understand that one of the influences or prongs may have more of an impact than the others. There is no cookie-cutter recipe for all youths. They are very much individuals despite their common behaviors. Throwing a large net of generalizations may not be an effective and efficient way to profile and understand the behavior of the acting-out child.

The day a threat is made, a preliminary assessment needs to be done on the threat. Information needs to be gathered on who is making the threat, what the threat is, and what is known about the individual, using the four-prong model. Information needs to be gathered, analyzed for seriousness, and identified as being high, medium, or low, and proper action needs to be taken by school authorities. At times very little is known about the possible shooter or offender, so gathering any type of information is paramount to action.

Below are several checklists that were developed by the author to help school staff look more closely at the students who are demonstrating troubling behaviors. These checklists were developed using the information from the FBI Threat Assessment Report. One response to the pressure for action around school shootings may be an effort to identify the next shooter by developing a "profile" of the typical school shooter.

This may sound like a reasonable preventive measure, but in practice, trying to draw up a catalogue or "checklist" of warning signs to detect a potential school shooter can be shortsighted. Such lists, publicized by the media, can end up unfairly labeling many nonviolent students as potentially dangerous or even lethal. In fact, a great many adolescents who will never commit violent acts will show some of the behaviors or personality traits included on the lists.

It is key that school officials use these checklists as a guide to begin discussion around providing the right kinds of interventions and support services. Using these checklists to diagnose a future school shooter would be unwise. If school officials have concerns around a certain student, these checklists can guide the observation process, help in the collection of relevant data, and assist in determining appropriate school action.

Personality of the Student: Behavior Characteristics and Traits

This checklist is to be used as a guide only; not all youths will demonstrate the following characteristics.

Frequency (F)	Duration (D)	Intensity (I)
a. Every 5 min.	a. 5 min.	a. Mild
b. Every 15 min.	b. 15 min.	b. Average
c. Hourly	c. 30 min.	c. Extreme
d. Daily	d. More than 30 min.	
e. Too frequent to count	e. More than 1 hour	

Characteristic	Present	F-D-I
1. Engages in strange behavior	Yes/No	(F)_____ (D)_____ (I)_____
2. Struggles with vulnerability	Yes/No	
3. Struggles with acceptance	Yes/No	(F)_____ (D)_____ (I)_____
4. Struggles with independence	Yes/No	(F)_____ (D)_____ (I)_____
5. Struggles with dependence	Yes/No	(F)_____ (D)_____ (I)_____
6. Difficulty with authority	Yes/No	(F)_____ (D)_____ (I)_____
7. Difficulty with coping with conflicts	Yes/No	(F)_____ (D)_____ (I)_____
8. Difficulty with disappointments	Yes/No	(F)_____ (D)_____ (I)_____ (F)_____ (D)_____ (I)_____
9. Difficulty with failures	Yes/N	(F)_____ (D)_____ (I)_____
10. Difficulty with insults	Yes/No	(F)_____ (D)_____ (I)_____
11. Many daily stressors encountered	Yes/No	(F)_____ (D)_____ (I)_____ (F)_____ (D)_____ (I)_____
12. Expresses anger and/or rage	Yes/No	(F)_____ (D)_____ (I)_____
13. Expresses frustration	Yes/No	(F)_____ (D)_____ (I)_____
14. Expresses disappointments	Yes/No	(F)_____ (D)_____ (I)_____
15. Encounters humiliation	Yes/N	(F)_____ (D)_____ (I)_____
16. Demonstrates sadness	Yes/No	(F)_____ (D)_____ (I)_____
17. Fails to demonstrate resiliency	Yes/No	(F)_____ (D)_____ (I)_____
18. Continuous setback	Yes/No	(F)_____ (D)_____ (I)_____
19. Encounters many failures	Yes/No	(F)_____ (D)_____ (I)_____
20. Overreaction to criticism	Yes/No	(F)_____ (D)_____ (I)_____
21. Difficulty with perceived criticism	Yes/No	(F)_____ (D)_____ (I)_____
22. Demonstrates low self-esteem	Yes/No	(F)_____ (D)_____ (I)_____
23. Inflated sense of self	Yes/No	(F)_____ (D)_____ (I)_____
24. Accurate sense of how others perceive them	Yes/No	(F)_____ (D)_____ (I)_____
25. Respects rules	Yes/No	(F)_____ (D)_____ (I)_____

26. Disrespects rules	Yes/No	(F)_____	(D)_____	(I)_____
27. Follows instructions	Yes/No	(F)_____	(D)_____	(I)_____
28. Non-compliant to instruction	Yes/No	(F)_____	(D)_____	(I)_____
29. Compliant to authority	Yes/No	(F)_____	(D)_____	(I)_____
30. Non-compliant to authority	Yes/No	(F)_____	(D)_____	(I)_____
31. Expresses a need for control	Yes/No	(F)_____	(D)_____	(I)_____
32. Expresses a need for attention	Yes/No	(F)_____	(D)_____	(I)_____
33. Expresses a need for respect	Yes/No	(F)_____	(D)_____	(I)_____
34. Expresses a need for admiration	Yes/No	(F)_____	(D)_____	(I)_____
35. Demonstrates confrontation	Yes/No	(F)_____	(D)_____	(I)_____
36. Fails to demonstrate empathy	Yes/No	(F)_____	(D)_____	(I)_____
37. Superior attitude toward others	Yes/No	(F)_____	(D)_____	(I)_____
38. Treats others as inferior	Yes/No	(F)_____	(D)_____	(I)_____
39. Demonstrates empathy	Yes/No	(F)_____	(D)_____	(I)_____
40. Many negative experiences	Yes/No	(F)_____	(D)_____	(I)_____
41. Leakage reveals clues to feelings	Yes/No	(F)_____	(D)_____	(I)_____
42. Subtle threats	Yes/No	(F)_____	(D)_____	(I)_____
43. Written notes/drawings	Yes/No	(F)_____	(D)_____	(I)_____
44. Involves others in preparations	Yes/No	(F)_____	(D)_____	(I)_____
45. Deceives friends and family	Yes/No	(F)_____	(D)_____	(I)_____
46. Failed love relationship	Yes/No	(F)_____	(D)_____	(I)_____
47. Resentment over injustices	Yes/No	(F)_____	(D)_____	(I)_____
48. Signs of depression	Yes/No	(F)_____	(D)_____	(I)_____
49. Signs of narcissism	Yes/No	(F)_____	(D)_____	(I)_____
50. Estranged from others	Yes/No	(F)_____	(D)_____	(I)_____
51. Dehumanizes others	Yes/No	(F)_____	(D)_____	(I)_____
52. Exaggerated sense of entitlement	Yes/No	(F)_____	(D)_____	(I)_____
53. Pathological need for attention	Yes/No	(F)_____	(D)_____	(I)_____
54. Externalizes blame	Yes/No	(F)_____	(D)_____	(I)_____
55. Anger management problems	Yes/No	(F)_____	(D)_____	(I)_____
56. Intolerance toward others	Yes/No	(F)_____	(D)_____	(I)_____

(*continued on next page*)

57. Inappropriate humor	Yes/No	(F)_____(D)_____(I)_____
58. Seeks to manipulate others	Yes/No	(F)_____(D)_____(I)_____
59. Lack of trust	Yes/No	(F)_____(D)_____(I)_____
60. Closed social group	Yes/No	(F)_____(D)_____(I)_____
61. Change in recent behaviors	Yes/No	(F)_____(D)_____(I)_____
62. Rigid and opinionated	Yes/No	(F)_____(D)_____(I)_____
63. Unusual interest in sensational violence	Yes/No	(F)_____(D)_____(I)_____
64. Fascination with violence-filled entertainment	Yes/No	(F)_____(D)_____(I)_____
65. Negative role models	Yes/No	(F)_____(D)_____(I)_____

Source: Adapted from FBI Threat Assessment report

Answer Criteria: Circle yes or no to each criterion/symptom if it has been observed for the categories shown in the box below.

Abbreviate (F) for Frequency, (D) Duration, and (I) Intensity.

Scoring: This checklist is to be used as a guide in the risk assessment of a threat situation. The people who work most closely with the child who has made the threat should have a good understanding of these personality dynamics. If a child demonstrates more than 50 percent of these characteristics you may have an at-risk individual on your hands. Of course there are many factors that influence a youth to shoot others, but this list of characteristics has been found as being present in some past shooters. One needs to be careful not to over-generalize these symptoms to all at-risk students.

It is interesting to note that teasing and physical fighting is more frequent at age thirteen to fourteen, while criminal activity generally peaks between fifteen and seventeen; the age of the individual will influence the likeliness of him or her using violence and/or using a gun to shoot others.

Also, adolescents are at risk for psychosocial problems and poor developmental outcomes such as academic failure, alcohol, drug abuse, delinquency, and problems with the law and violence. These other factors also play a role in the possibility that an individual will use a weapon to commit a crime.

Family Dynamics

Family dynamics are patterns of behavior, thinking, beliefs, traditions, roles, and customs that exist in a family. When there is an issue with a child who has made a threat, it is important to have some idea of what factors may be present in this child's family background. The factors that may lead to a crisis are listed below in the checklist developed for that purpose. It is important to state that the dynamics perceived by the child, parents, and school officials are instrumental in understanding whether the child will carry out the threat or not. Family dynamics have a way of integrating themselves into all aspects of the individual's life; the moment that a child reaches critical mass of these dynamics may be the trigger that sets the course of events into action.

Family Dynamics Checklist

Below is a checklist of characteristics that may be present in an at-risk individual's family background. One must be aware that not all youths and children that match this profile will become shooters or will use violence as a means to obtain what they desire.

Answer Criteria: Circle yes or no to each criterion/symptom if it has been observed.

Scoring: If there are more than fifteen to twenty of these indicators in a child's life, there is reason for concern. It is not a guarantee that a child will become a shooter with these characteristics in his life, but there is definitely family dysfunction that may lead to other behaviors. These other behaviors may take the form of petty crimes and/or property vandalism and

Characteristics	Observed or Present
1. Difficult parental relationship	Yes/No
2. Recent multiple moves	Yes/No
3. Loss of a parent	Yes/No
4. Addition of a step-parent	Yes/No
5. Expresses contempt for parents	Yes/No
6. Rejects parents in his life	Yes/No
7. Rejects roles of parents	Yes/No
8. Violence within the home	Yes/No
9. Parental reaction to behavior is minimal	Yes/No
10. Parents do not find behavior abnormal	Yes/No
11. Parents are unable to recognize or acknowledge behavior as a concern	Yes/No
12. Parents react defensively to criticism	Yes/No
13. Parents confrontational with school officials	Yes/No
14. Parents seem unconcerned	Yes/No
15. Parents minimize reports	Yes/No
16. Parents reject any reports on misbehavior	Yes/No
17. Guns are present in the home	Yes/No
18. Weapons are kept in the home	Yes/No
19. Explosives are in the home	Yes/No
20. Weapons are treated carelessly	Yes/No
21. No safety precautions taken with weapons	Yes/No
22. Guns are loaded	Yes/No
23. Parents model careless use of weapons	Yes/No
24. Parents demonstrate use of weapons to solve conflicts	Yes/No
25. Family lacks closeness	Yes/No
26. No family intimacy	Yes/No
27. Frequent moves	Yes/No
28. Family has recently relocated	Yes/No
29. Parents set few rules	Yes/No
30. No code of conduct for child	Yes/No
31. Parents give in to child's demands	Yes/No
32. Child insists on inordinate amount of privacy	Yes/No
33. Parents have little information about friends	Yes/No
34. Parents have little information on whereabouts	Yes/No
35. Parents have little information on activities	Yes/No
36. Parents have little information on school life	Yes/No
37. Parents have little information on relationships	Yes/No
38. Parents are intimidated by child	Yes/No

39.	Parents fear child will attack them physically	Yes/No
40.	Parents unwilling to face emotional outbursts	Yes/No
41.	Traditional family roles are reversed	Yes/No
42.	No limits on television watching	Yes/No
43.	No limits on internet usage	Yes/No
44.	No defined times for activity with others	Yes/No
45.	Is secretive about computer use	Yes/No
46.	Plays violent games on the internet	Yes/No
47.	Researches violent sites on internet	Yes/No
48.	Researches weapons on internet	Yes/No
49.	Parents are unable to access child's computer	Yes/No
50.	Drugs and alcohol present	Yes/No

Source: Adapted from the FBI Threat Assessment Report

theft. The combination of both personality and family dynamics coming together create an ambiance rich for disaster. Shooters have a tendency to resort to violence when they have nothing to care about in their lives. When there are no redeeming factors or people in one's life, it becomes easier to shoot and kill.

School Dynamics

School dynamics are patterns of behavior, thinking, beliefs, customs, traditions, roles, and values that exist in a school's culture. The only way to understand the culture of a school is to spend some time there. One cannot understand the structure, climate, and ambiance without having been there. Identifying which values, behaviors, and expectations are valued and reinforced must be accomplished before doing a risk assessment.

Some schools do a wonderful job of explaining to students how they can be successful and get approval and acceptance from both school officials and their peers, while others are more ambiguous about how to achieve those desired outcomes. For some students, when they understand these expectations they are more able to fit in and be part of the group, while others have a much more difficult time and are more likely to become isolated or ostracized.

The group that becomes ostracized and not able to fit in with the school's values and beliefs is the one more likely to resort to violence. Lack of connection to the staff of the school also is important in understanding the system and culture of that particular school. Students and staff may have very different perspectives and perceptions on the culture and values of the school.

In any type of assessment it is important to have a very good handle on how students see their school. Discrepancy between staff and students can be key in understanding the reasons why a school may be under attack. Below is a checklist of indicators that assess the dynamics of a school's potential to experiencing a shooting crisis. These criteria are to be used to self-evaluate by school officials as well as those who may be assessing the situation at the time of the crisis.

School Dynamics Checklist

The following is a list of criteria that may indicate that a school may be more likely to experience violence within its halls. This list is not exhaustive and not all schools with these criteria will have a school shooting.

Answer Criteria: Circle yes or no to each criterion/symptom if it has been observed.

Scoring: If ten or more of these criteria are present then the school has an environment that may make it a target. Administrators and school officials must begin the dialogue around making their school safer and more secure. In discussions with student groups and staff, issues can be put on the table that will hopefully lead to a proactive change in school culture and may prevent the disaster of a school shooting!

Characteristics	Observed-Present
1. Student is detached from school	Yes/No
2. Student is detached from others	Yes/No
3. Student is detached from teachers	Yes/No
4. School does very little to address behaviors	Yes/No
5. School does very little to prevent disrespectful behaviors	Yes/No
6. Bullying is part of school culture	Yes/No
7. School authorities are oblivious to bullying	Yes/No
8. Bullying interventions are inconsistent	Yes/No
9. Students act in the role of a bully	Yes/No
10. Student act in the role of a victim	Yes/No
11. Students are bystanders to bullying	Yes/No
12. School atmosphere promotes racial issues	Yes/No
13. School atmosphere promotes social class divisions	Yes/No
14. Use of discipline is inequitably applied to students	Yes/No
15. Use of discipline is inequitably applied by staff	Yes/No
16. School culture is static	Yes/No
17. School culture is unyielding	Yes/No
18. School culture is insensitive to changes in society	Yes/No
19. School culture is insensitive to new students and faculty	Yes/No
20. Certain groups of students given prestige over others	Yes/No
21. Certain groups are not given respect by school officials	Yes/No
22. Code of silence prevails in student body	Yes/No
23. Few students feel safe to talk to staff about issues	Yes/No
24. Little trust exists between students and staff	Yes/No
25. Access to computers is unsupervised or unmonitored	Yes/No
26. Students can use school computers to play violent games	Yes/No
27. Students are allowed to visit hate and violent internet sites	Yes/No
28. Poor home and school communication	Yes/No
29. Poor community relationships between school and families	Yes/No
30. Lack of proper security and safety precautions	Yes/No

Source: Adapted from the FBI Threat Assessment Report

Social Dynamics

Social dynamics are patterns of behavior, thinking, beliefs, customs, traditions, and roles that exist in the larger community where students live. These patterns have an impact on students' behaviors, their feelings about themselves, their outlook on life, attitudes, perceived options, and lifestyle practices. What a young person believes about his or her community is what is found in that community.

If the child is surrounded by drugs, alcohol, poverty, and weapons, then she begins to act accordingly and will reflect in some fashion the social dynamics of the community where she lives and goes to school. Within this community, peer groups play a huge role in influencing attitudes and behavior. Information about a child's friends and relationships with peers and or classmates can provide clues to his attitudes, sense of identity, whether he will act out or not, and whether the threat is just a threat or it is a plan of action waiting to be executed.

The following is a checklist to monitor and evaluate the role that social dynamics play in the possibility of a student acting out in a violent manner.

Social Dynamics

This checklist can be used to evaluate the possible influences that a child may have in his community that will put him more at risk.

Answer Criteria: Circle yes or no to each criterion/symptom if it has been observed for the categories.

Scoring: If there are five to seven of these criteria met, then intervention is necessary. These societal factors will not guarantee that an individual will become a school shooter but it is more likely that the individual may resort to some sort of violence.

Reliably predicting any type of violence is extremely difficult. Predicting that an individual who has never acted out vi-

Characteristics	Observed or Present
1. Easy and unmonitored access to movies	Yes/No
2. Unmonitored access to internet sites	Yes/No
3. Visits violent internet sites/violent games	Yes/No
4. Individual is involved with a group that shares a fascination with violence	Yes/No
5. Individual is involved with a group that has extremist beliefs and actions	Yes/No
6. Extremist groups isolate individuals	Yes/No
7. Individual is always with extremist group	Yes/No
8. Individual becomes defensive when challenged on beliefs	Yes/No
9. Individual lacks reality check	Yes/No
10. Individual uses drugs and alcohol	Yes/No
11. Individual expresses strong attitudes about drugs and alcohol	Yes/No
12. Behavior changes are present due to drugs and alcohol	Yes/No
13. Outside school interests are focused on violence	Yes/No
14. Individual has no outside interests	Yes/No
15. Copycat behaviors from media are present	Yes/No
16. Individual refers to other school shootings	Yes/No
17. Individual worships a school shooter	Yes/No
18. Individual threatens school shooting	Yes/No
19. Individual has a plan of action for violence	Yes/No
20. Individual has written a suicide note	Yes/No

Source: Adapted from the FBI Threat Assessment Report.

olently in the past will do so in the future is still more difficult. Seeking to predict acts that occur as rarely as school shootings is almost impossible. This is simple statistical logic: When the incidence of any form of violence is very low and a very large number of people have identifiable risk factors, there is no reliable way to pick out from that large group the very few who will actually commit the violent act.

The checklists presented in this chapter do not diagnose or predict that a student will become a school shooter. It would be foolish to think that one could accurately predict with certainty that a student would become a shooter. These checklists are to be used to begin the discussion around the issues that may be facing certain individuals within our school populations. The discussions that may occur around the findings of the checklists may lead to proactive psychological and social interventions for a child.

After a violent incident has taken place, retracing an offender's past and identifying clues that in retrospect could have been signs of danger can yield significant, useful information.

However, even clues that appear to help interpret past events should not be taken as predictors of similar events in the future. At this time, there is no research that has identified traits and characteristics that can reliably distinguish school shooters from other students.

Many students appear to have traits and characteristics similar to those observed in students who were involved in school shootings. It seems that a combination of factors and life events must come together to create the environment that will lead to a school shooting. Thank God they are few and far between. The important piece in this chapter's discussions is to know that we need to be more aware of the factors that students live with day to day. It will be imperative that schools become more able to recognize and self-evaluate their own performance around creating environments that are safe, secure, and welcoming places. There is much work to be done in this domain.

4

Bullying: Personal and Cyberspace

Definition

Bullying is defined as the act of intentionally causing harm to others through verbal harassment, physical assault, or other more subtle methods of coercion such as manipulation. Bullying is an act of repeated aggressive behavior in order to intentionally hurt another person. Bullying is about power. Bullying can take many forms: name calling, verbal or written abuse, exclusion from activities, exclusion from social situations, physical abuse, and coercion.

Bullying has made its way into the newspaper headlines and therefore school officials need to address the problem. For years students have been bullied in silence. The victims were quiet due to intense fear of repercussions, while the bully was able to continue with very few consequences. In fact, it is the victim's silence that has fostered the belief in the bully that bullying is acceptable behavior and a victim just needs to live with it.

Major findings presented in the research on bullying behavior include the following:

- American schools harbor approximately 2.1 million bullies and 2.7 million victims.
- It is estimated that nearly 160,000 students miss school each day due to fear of attack or intimidation.
- Bullied students are apt to tell a family member or friend of the abuse, but rarely a teacher or an administrator.
- Young bullies carry a one-in-four chance of having a criminal record by the age of thirty.
- Bullying can be reduced as much as 50 percent with the implementation of an effective bullying prevention program.
- Effective bullying prevention programs include a needs assessment, student, staff, and community components, and an effective communications plan.
- Antibullying interventions are unlikely to work unless they are part of a school or school-district-based comprehensive program.
- Consistent use of consequences is a necessary component of effective prevention.
- Ongoing education is most effective after a system of consequences is firmly in place. A program should be aimed at the silent student majority (the 85 percent who are neither victims nor bullies).
- Structured counseling and education for bullies that stresses acknowledging actions and restitution is likely to be effective if it follows negative consequences for bullying behavior. (Center for Professional Development, 2007)

It Is Bullying When

A person willfully subjects another person (victim), whoever he or she may be, to an intentional, unwanted, and unprovoked hurtful verbal and/or physical action(s), which results in the victim feeling oppressed (stress, injury, discomfort) or threatened at any school site, school bus, or school board–sponsored activity or event. Bullying is a form of aggression.

Examples or types of bullying may include, but are not limited to:

- *Physical bullying*—punching, shoving, poking, strangling, hair pulling, beating, biting, excessive tickling, tripping, and pinching.
- *Verbal bullying*—such acts as hurtful name calling, racial slurs, threats, taunts, insults, teasing, and gossip.
- *Emotional (psychological) bullying*—rejecting, terrorizing, extorting, defaming, humiliating, blackmailing, rating/ranking of personal characteristics such as race, disability, ethnicity, or perceived sexual orientation, manipulating friendships, isolating, ostracizing, and peer pressure.
- *Sexual bullying*—many of the actions listed above as well as exhibitionism, voyeurism, sexual propositioning, sexual harassment, and abuse involving actual physical contact and sexual assault. In many cases, gender and cross-gender sexual harassment may also qualify as bullying.
- *Cyberbullying*—tormenting, threatening, taunting, ranking, degrading a target, harassing, humiliating, or otherwise targeting a student or staff member using the Internet, interactive and digital technologies, or mobile phones or inviting others to join in these acts.

There are three essential components to any bullying situation. There must be a bully, a victim, and a location in which it can occur. The fourth component is bystanders, who can play a role in encouraging the bully or protecting the victim. Bullying can be indirect or direct. Direct bullying is usually in your face, where the victim is physically harmed in some way. Indirect bullying is where the victim is attacked through gossip, rumors, writing, or instant messages, and their reputation is tarnished in some way.

Regarding gender, boys are more likely to engage in direct bullying and girls in indirect bullying. The bully usually will possess levels of self-esteem that are as positive as their non-bully peers. Some bullies do not have empathy as part of their repertoire of skills and may actually enjoy hurting others.

There is no single descriptive profile of a child who is at risk for being bullied. Children who are socially isolated are easier targets because they lack a social network of friends to protect them. There are two subgroups of bully victims: the passive victims and the provocative victims. Passive victims are weaker physically, avoid confrontations, and generally are more anxious.

Provocative victims are anxious and aggressive. They are more confrontational and tend to irritate or alienate their classmates. These children often explode quickly and are easy targets. Bullying is a covert activity and adults rarely see it happening. Single teachers alone in a classroom rarely are able to pick up on the bullying occurring within that environment.

Locations are key to the action of bullying. Bullies are opportunistic, preying on weaker students when there is no adult supervision. The far corner of a classroom, a deserted hallway, the bathrooms, or any area that is poorly supervised make for a great zone for bullying behaviors.

Bystanders, those who observe the bullying, are more likely to encourage the bully than to attempt to help the victim. They do not remain neutral. They often will applaud the bully or be thankful that it is not them being bullied. This behavior is common in our society. The Good Samaritan is no longer the right thing to do in American society; it is easier and safer to walk away. This is sad, but a reality of the world in the twenty-first century.

Strategies for Prevention of Bullying in Schools

1. Adopt policies that address bullying behavior focused on assisting students to increase self-control and take positive responsibilities for their actions.
2. Build a school climate that builds trust and support by demonstrating respect for all.
3. Conduct an annual survey to assist and inform school staff, students, and parents in identifying antibullying strategies to be implemented at the school site.
4. Discuss the problem of bullying openly with students and gather their input on the seriousness of the problem and possible solutions.
5. Provide staff training on how to identify and respond to bullying behavior.
6. Increase staff supervision in areas where bullying behavior is likely to occur.
7. Organize a bank of resources that can assist with bullying problems and offer practical solutions. Identify national and local experts who can speak on the topic in a compelling way.
8. Recognize, celebrate, and acknowledge students and other groups who are making a positive difference in the school in reducing bullying behavior.
9. Check if there is a staff education system in place to assist in the identification of bullying behavior and a monitoring system to make sure that consequences and education are effective.
10. Check if there is a system in place that ensures that students know how to identify and respond to bullying behavior.
11. Determine if parent and community organizations are supporting school efforts to reduce bullying behavior.
12. Compile a menu of appropriate consequences for bullying behaviors.

13. Establish a policy for contacting parents of children who engage in bullying.
14. Monitor the school's prevention efforts on an ongoing basis.
15. Teachers must assess the extent of the bullying problem in their classroom.
16. Teachers must ensure that the class understands what bullying is and why it is wrong.
17. Teachers must confront any student engaged in bullying in a firm but fair manner.
18. Teachers must provide appropriate and consistent consequences for bullying.
19. Teachers must drop by unexpectedly to observe their class in less structured environments.
20. Teachers must watch for patterns of bullying individuals or groups of students.
21. Teachers need to be on the lookout for prolonged teasing, name calling, and any verbal harassment.
22. Teachers must interact with other school staff to communicate concerns about either the victims or the bullies.
23. Teachers must define and have a common understanding with their students of what bullying entails.
24. Teachers can hold class meetings and come up with appropriate rules and expectations.
25. Teachers need to address the problem of bullying immediately. This should be done in private—rarely should this be done publicly. And it should be conducted in a brief and businesslike manner.
26. Teachers can find mentors for bullies that may help in changing behaviors and address some of the core issues around the reasons a child may be bullying.
27. Teachers can develop a reward chart to shape the bully's behavior in a more positive direction.

Strategies to Help the Victim

Children who are bullied are often unhappy in school, suffer from low self-esteem, and are isolated from their peers. They often are rejected socially, which in turn affects their sense of self and academic performance. The way victims can be helped is for a school to have a schoolwide bully prevention program.

The following are some suggestions to help victims deal with the bullying:

1. Take steps to ensure the victim's safety.
2. Have the child fill out an anonymous questionnaire that asks where, who, and when the bullying has occurred.
3. Increase supervision in areas known for attacks.
4. Create a safe room that is staffed by adults (study hall, counselor's office, resource room).
5. Examine the victim's daily schedule to find blind spots and unsupervised places and times the child may be alone.
6. Ensure the child has at least one friend with her at all times.
7. Help build the social standing of the child within the class group, school group, and community.
8. Train socially inept children in basic social skills.
9. Train the child how to ask to be included in games or social situations.
10. Pair students for random interactive learning and leisure activities.
11. Change the seating chart in a classroom periodically to foster friendships.
12. Make sure the child is involved in class free-time activities.
13. Have a mentor for the child so that he can speak openly to that person.

14. Teach assertiveness skills.
15. Teach the child to maintain his composure, stand firm, and continue to behave appropriately even when provoked.
16. Teach the child to respond to taunts and teasing with bland responses.
17. Teach the child to leave the situation if starting to get angry or fearful.
18. Teach the child how to say no loudly.
19. Teach the child how to posture assertiveness and confidence through role-playing.
20. Teach the child how to deal with peer pressure.
21. Teach the child to report incidences immediately to an adult.

Locations: Transforming Schools to Safe Havens—Strategies

Bullying takes place in a variety of environments. The bully must have a setting or location that is adult-free so that he can exploit or intimidate his victim. Bullying occurs in deserted or unsupervised areas.

The following are a list of recommendations to prevent bullying in some locations:

1. Teachers should be a physical presence in the school.
2. The school uncovers the hotspots in the school and community where the bullying is occurring regularly.
3. Teachers go on a school tour with their students to identify safe and unsafe areas.
4. Students identify times of day the above areas are safe and unsafe.
5. Students are given community maps of the surrounding neighborhoods and asked to identify unsafe and safe places.

6. The above information should be shared with local police or resource officers.
7. Increase adult supervision in stairwells, hallways, and playgrounds.
8. Student peer monitors walk in these areas regularly.
9. Help the adults learn student names so that there can be a personal connection.
10. Separate older and younger students when they are in less supervised areas.
11. Train noninstructional staff to intervene when they see bullying behaviors.
12. Increase the natural surveillance of areas in the school.
13. Change the classroom layout or rearrange seating to eliminate blind spots.
14. Teachers need to circulate frequently.
15. Put up antibullying posters in the hallways and stairways.
16. Create personal spaces for students.

Action Steps for Children

Classroom discussions may help students develop a variety of appropriate actions that they can take when bullying crosses their path.

1. Seek immediate help from adults.
2. Report bullying/victimization to school personnel.
3. Speak up and/or support the victim when they see her being bullied.
4. Privately support those being hurt with words of kindness.
5. Express disapproval of bullying behavior by not joining in the laughter, teasing, or spreading of rumors and gossip.
6. Attempt to defuse problem situations either single-handedly or in a group.

Action Steps for Parents

When children are involved in bullying situations, it is crucial that the parents take notice and become aware of what may be happening. It is important that parents have open lines of communication with their children. The children must be able to approach parents with their concerns so that parents are then able to address with appropriate responses to the bullying behaviors experienced by their child at school.

1. Make sure the child does not believe that he is to blame for the bullying and that he understands the bully's behavior is the source of the problem, not him as a person.
2. Call the school. Work collaboratively with school personnel.
3. Keep records of incidents so that you can be specific in your discussions with school personnel.
4. Arrange meetings with a school counselor, principal, or class teacher. Are they aware of the issues? Do they have firsthand knowledge of the situation?
5. Do not speak directly to the bullying child.
6. If speaking with the parents of the bully, be careful in the approach; this may turn violent, as many parents of bullies are bullies themselves.
7. Do not encourage your child to become aggressive and strike back.
8. Teach your child to be assertive and to use humor if appropriate.
9. Be patient—conflict between children is rarely solved overnight.
10. Spend time with your child to process the emotions and situations.
11. Help your child develop new interests or strengthen existing talents and skills that help develop and improve self-esteem.

12. If the problem persists or worsens, consult an attorney, contact local police, and press charges.

Cyberbullying: Meanness Goes Online!

Bullying has reformatted itself to keep up with the times. Long gone are the times when bullies existed only on the playground or in your neighborhood, harassing you on the ballpark or while you were walking home from school. Bullying has become technological. Tech-savvy students are turning to cyberspace to harass their peers. In a United Kingdom report, one in four children, some as young as eleven years old, are bullied in Great Britain. A Canadian study reports that 13 percent of students are bullied monthly. A U.S. study says that one in seventeen youngsters between the ages of ten and seventeen has been threatened or harassed online (Phi Delta Kappa, 2007).

Cyberbullying is defined as willful and repeated harm inflicted through the medium of electronic text (Patchin & Hinduja, 2006). Traditional bullying involves threatening, pushing, fighting, and violence. Traditional bullying is associated with malicious intent, using intimidation, and having a power differential between aggressor and victim. Cyberbullies exist because they can use a medium that creates fear by the tapping of a keyboard key.

One can assume that the cyberbully is a malicious aggressor who is seeking some sort of power, control, or revenge. Somehow she is receiving pleasure in the form of watching the chaos and mental anguish that is being caused, or for some reason she may profit from her efforts. Cyberbullying involves harmful behaviors that are of a repetitive nature and can become addictive to some personality types.

The power gained from destroying lives can be intoxicating. The nature of this type of bullying maintains some perceived or actual power over their victims. Bullies are often cowards and manipulative as well as fearful, so what better way to intimidate or take control than to navigate the electronic world in a way that they continue to exert their power? Many have discovered that when you are physically present and you are violent, other people see your actions and you are more likely to be caught. In the World Wide Web you only get caught if you are not technologically aware, or if you make a stupid mistake.

There are two main ways cyberbullies harass: on the Internet they use chat rooms, bulletin boards, websites, e-mails, MySpace, and so on, and off the Internet, cellular phones and text messages. One thing is certain: it is very difficult to apprehend cyberbullies. They can virtually be anonymous. Many offenders develop temporary e-mail accounts, pseudonyms, and instant messaging programs and can hide in plain sight.

There are many tricks. It is interesting to note that once a strategy to bully has been discovered, there is a new way around it. Technology in all its glory and its need to be progressive makes it more difficult to catch the perpetrators. Since it is harder to be caught on the Internet, bullies become emboldened, because it takes less energy to type, to accuse, and to threaten than it does to use one's voice.

Another key element in cyberbullying is that there are very few monitors in chat rooms and websites. Freedom of expression laws have allowed people to post and say whatever they desire and adolescents do not have the ability to self-monitor and self-regulate with any level of consistency and accuracy. And since this generation is more proficient than the adults in their lives, they can circumvent any adult or parental interventions due to the limited knowledge of those adults. Parents are often unaware of their child's activity—whether the child is a bully or a victim.

Cell phones have now become an appendage to many people's lives. This unfortunately makes all who possess a cell phone a potential victim, never free of the potential dangers of being victimized. The sad part is that groups of adolescents can coordinate a bullying attack with ease. Since the bullies do not have to be present, coordination can happen anywhere in the world. The results can be devastating for victims.

Attacks from all aspects of the person's life can be overwhelming and lead to self-destruction or acting-out behaviors. Bullies often send text messages involving sex, sexual orientation, or race comments. Boys seem to be victims of homophobic harassments, racial slurs, and threats of violence. Girls are often victims of unwelcome sexual comments and threats of sexual abuse.

Two such examples include a girl who broke up with her boyfriend only to find out that her ex superimposed her face on a pornographic Internet picture and distributed it to the whole school, and an overweight male student who had his picture taken while changing in a locker room, and the picture was subsequently sent throughout the school, causing humiliation and grief. The consequences can be very serious, with victims suffering in terms of their schoolwork and self-esteem, and many drop out of school because of attacks. Some even commit suicide.

Statistics

In a study conducted in 2005 by Sameer Hinduja and Justin Patchin, results indicated the following: 1,500 Internet-using adolescents reported experiences with cyberbulling—80 percent reported online bullying; 32 percent of males and 36 percent of females reported being bullied; 40 percent were disrespected; 12 percent were threatened; 5 percent were scared for their safety; and 56 percent bullied in chat rooms—49 percent in computer text messages and 28 percent via e-mail; 40 percent told no one of the bullying (www.cyberbullying.us).

Other studies indicated the following results: 18 percent of students in grades six through eight said they had been cyberbullied at least once in the last couple of months and

6 percent said it had happened to them two or more times (Kowalski et al., 2005). Eleven percent of students in grades six through eight said they had cyberbullied another person at least once in the last couple of months and 2 percent said they had done it two or more times (Kowalski et al., 2005). Nineteen percent of regular Internet users between the ages of ten and seventeen reported being involved in online aggression; 15 percent had been aggressors and 7 percent had been targets (3 percent were both aggressors and targets) (Ybarra & Mitchell, 2004). Seventeen percent of six- to eleven-year-olds and thirty-six percent of twelve- to seventeen-year-olds reported that someone said threatening or embarrassing things about them through e-mail, instant messages, websites, chat rooms, or text messages (Fight Crime: Invest in Kids, 2006).

Cyberbullying has increased in recent years. In nationally representative surveys of ten- to seventeen-year-olds, twice as many children and youth indicated that they had been victims and perpetrators of online harassment in 2005 compared with 1999/2000 (Wolak, Mitchell & Finkelhor, 2006).

Warning Signs

Several indicators exist for parents and educators to know if a child is being bullied as well as bullying others. This list is not exhaustive and is only a start to identification of the issue.

Being Bullied—Victims

1. Child stops using the computer.
2. Appears nervous or jumpy when an instant message or e-mail appears.
3. Appears uneasy about going to school or outside in general.
4. Appears to be angry, depressed, or frustrated after using the computer.

5. Avoids discussions about what they are doing on the computer.
6. Becomes abnormally withdrawn from usual friends and family members.
7. Withdrawal from friends or activities.
8. Drop in academic performance.
9. Child is a target of traditional bullying at school.
10. Child appears depressed or sad. (Kowalski et al. 2007; Willard, 2006)

Cyberbullying—Those Who Are Doing the Bullying

1. Quickly switches screens or closes programs when you walk by.
2. Uses computer at all hours of the night.
3. Gets unusually upset if she cannot use the computer.
4. Laughs excessively while using the computer.
5. Avoids discussions about what he is doing on the computer.
6. Is using multiple online accounts, or an account that is not her own. (Patchin and Hinduja, 2006)

Strategies and Recommendations for Educators and Parents

At times, parents may feel helpless in discovering what is wrong with their adolescent. Adolescents in general may be moody, reactive, hyper, withdrawn, and emotional. So how do parents know that their child is being bullied and what can they do about it? The list below includes some suggestions for parents to use if they are dealing with an adolescent who may be a target of electronic bullying. This list is not exhaustive, but includes recommendations of starting points or interventions that may lead to ending the bullying.

Parents

1. Communicate. Keep everyone talking about what is happening on the computer and cell phones. Internet filters do not protect against cyberbullies. Make sure that the affected student has strategies to talk about it and do some problem solving. Peer support can be key as other youths can help with problem-solving options and solutions. Community and parental involvement can minimize online bullying.
2. Encourage openness. Bullies function in secrecy. They do their best work of intimidation and humiliation when no one is watching. They hope that their victim will keep quiet and isolated. Openness is one solution because telling parents, teachers, and supportive adults can make the bullying stop or at least reduce the impact of verbal harassment. Talk regularly with your child about online activities he or she is involved in. Talk specifically about cyberbullying and encourage your child to tell you immediately if he is the victim of cyberbullying, cyberstalking, or other illegal or troublesome online behavior. Encourage your child to tell you if she is aware of others who may be the victims of such behavior. Explain that cyberbullying is harmful and unacceptable behavior. Outline your expectations for responsible online behavior and make it clear that there will be consequences for inappropriate behavior.
3. Engagement of the bully. This is very difficult for many youths. The function of the behavior of the bully is to get attention and get a reaction from the victim. Lack of response or ignoring the behavior may help to extinguish the harassment. However, one needs to be careful in this area, as some bullies will escalate their behavior till they get a response. If this occurs, a phone call to the local authorities may be necessary.

4. Monitoring of e-mail, Internet, and cell phone use. Parents need to be aware of their children's electronic activity. They need to decide when the youth is mature enough to handle the electronic devices. Adults need to consistently monitor online chat room visits, track IM discussion records, and help their child be responsible and accountable for what she says and writes on these electronic tools.

5. Bullies must be made responsible. Electronic bullying is a punishable offense. When bullies are caught, the victims must press criminal charges regardless of the age of the aggressor. Cyberbullies must be held accountable for all of their actions. Schools must become more vigilant and enforce their antibullying policies.

6. Keep your home computer(s) in easily viewable places, such as a family room or kitchen. Although adults must respect the privacy of children and youth, concerns for children's safety may sometimes override these privacy concerns. Tell your child that you may review his online communications if you think there is reason for concern.

7. Do not erase messages or pictures—save these as evidence.

8. Try to identify the individual doing the cyberbullying even if the cyberbully is anonymous. If cyberbullying is coming through e-mail or a cell phone, it may be possible to block future contact from the cyberbully.

9. Contact your school if cyberbullying is occurring through your school district's Internet system.

10. Consider contacting the cyberbully's parents if the bully is known, and proceed cautiously. If you decide to contact a cyberbully's parents, communicate with them in writing—not face-to-face. Present proof of the cyberbullying (e.g., copies of an e-mail message) and ask them to make sure the cyberbullying stops.

11. Consider contacting an attorney in cases of serious cyberbullying. In some circumstances, civil law permits victims to sue a bully or her parents in order to recover damages.

12. Contact the police if cyberbullying involves acts such as threats of violence, extortion, obscene or harassing phone calls or text messages, harassment, stalking, hate crimes, or child pornography. If you are uncertain if cyberbullying violates your jurisdiction's criminal laws, contact your local police who will advise you (Kowalski, 2005).

13. What kind of information should be saved? To report cyberbullying, it's really important to save as much information as you can. The more you have saved, the easier it will be to track down the people bothering you.

14. Save the following from e-mail:
    • E-mail address,
    • Date and time received, and
    • Copies of any relevant e-mail with full e-mail headers.

15. Save the following from groups or communities:
    • URL of offending group site,
    • Nickname of offending person,
    • E-mail address of offending person, and
    • Date you saw it happen.

16. Save the following from profiles you see on the Internet:
    • URL of profile,
    • Nickname of offending person,
    • E-mail address of offending person, and
    • Date you viewed this profile.

17. Save the following from chat rooms:
    • Date and time of chat,
    • Name and URL of chat room you were in,
    • Nickname of offending person,

- E-mail address of offending person, and
- Screenshot of chat room. (www.cyberbullying.us)

Suggestions for Educators

The place where youths spend the most time is at school. This is where cyberbullying finds its roots and develops. It is due to social conflicts at the school that students become targets. The upheaval of adolescence creates little monsters that will become mean due to several factors. Educators must be aware of the nuances and changes in behavior on the part of their students both for perpetrator and victim.

It is important that teachers have an excellent handle on the pulse of what is going on in the classroom. Being able to pay attention and listen for clues may save many hours of anguish on the part of the victim. Responsible adults must be present to monitor and supervise consistently. Here are several recommendations for schools and educators.

1. Educate your students, teachers, and other staff members about cyberbullying, its dangers, and what to do if someone is cyberbullied.
2. Make sure that your school's antibullying rules and policies address cyberbullying.
3. Closely monitor students' use of computers at school. Use filtering and tracking software on all computers, but don't rely solely on this software to screen out cyberbullying and other problematic online behavior.
4. Investigate reports of cyberbullying immediately. If it occurs through the school district's Internet system, you are obligated to take action. If it occurs off-campus, *consider what actions you might take* to help address the bullying: Notify parents of victims and parents of known or suspected cyberbullies.

5. Notify the police if known or suspected cyberbullying involves a threat. Closely monitor the behavior of the affected student(s) at school for possible bullying.
6. Talk with all students about the harms caused by cyberbullying. Remember that cyberbullying that occurs off-campus can travel like wildfire among your students and can affect how they behave and relate to each other at school.
7. Investigate to see if the victim(s) of cyberbullying could use some support from a school counselor or school-based mental health professional (Kowalski, 2005).
8. Hold classroom discussions in morning meetings about the effects of bullying.
9. Do role-plays and problem-solving exercises around bullying.
10. Teach students to be active reporters of bullying. Help them understand that being a bystander is an act of omission. They need to be involved in helping victims by speaking up.

Putting It All Together

We are all hoping for a school and world without bullying. It is a dream that can become a reality, whether it is on a school playground or in the world of politics. Bullying is everyone's problem: bullies at school become bullies in the workplace, relationships, and in the community. The cycle continues over generations unless we take a stand and start teaching young children and adolescents that those behaviors and actions will not be tolerated in our schools and in our lives. Only training children to think differently will influence their actions.

Educating and teaching children to become responsible for all their behaviors will commence the transformation that needs to occur. Will bullying ever disappear? It is a hope! However, it must begin with what is acceptable in terms of behaviors in American society. The government cannot go invading other countries or bully smaller nations into compliance to get economic growth and development. Children learn by example, so let us hope that the examples of the leaders of this country will be a positive and humanistic one. Future generations hopefully will have the benefit of our mistakes and do things differently.

Resources

Websites

"Bully B'ware," www.bullybeware.com

"Bully Free Kids," www.bullyfreekids.com

"Bullying. No way" (Australia), www.bullyingnoway.com

"Bullying.org, where no one is alone," (Canada) www.bullying.org

"Bully Police U.S.A.," www.bullypolice.org

"Childline" (United Kingdom), www.childline.org.uk

"Coalition for children," www.safechild.org

"Don't suffer in silence," www.dfes.gov.uk/bullying/index.shtml

"National Bullying Prevention Campaign," www.stopbullyingnow.hrsa.gov

"No bullying," Hazelden, www.hazelden.org

"Parent's point of view," www.jaredstory.com

"Safeguarding your children at school," www.pta.org/programs/sycsch.htm

"Steps to respect: A bully prevention program," The Committee for Children, www.cfchildren.org

"Stop Bullying Now," www.stopbullyingnow.com

"The Stop Bullying Project." www.stopbullyingnow.com

Books

The bully free classroom, A.L. Beane
The bully, the bullied and the bystander from preschool to high school, by B. Coloreso
Stop the bullying: A handbook for schools, by K. Rigby
The schoolyard bully: How to cope with conflict and raise an assertive child, by K. Zarzour

Videos

The broken toy, by Thomas Brown
Bully breath: How to tame a troublemaker, by the National Center for Violence Prevention
Bullying at school, by the Toronto School Board of Education
Don't pick on me, by the National Center for Violence Prevention
Let's get real, by Women's Educational Media
No more teasing, by the National Center for Violence Prevention
Real people: what hate is all about, by Sunburst Communications
Sticks and stones and stereotypes, by Equity Institute

5

Family Violence: The Seeds Are Planted Early

It is true we do not pick which family to be born into. The experiences of our early childhood form our personality and therefore create a well-adjusted individual or create a pathological antisocial individual. The rate of acting-out behaviors that have some sort of violent act has been increasing over the last thirty years. What is causing this? Is it environment, biology, or parenting? It would be very easy to play the "Blame the Parents" game, but I will not do that in this text. Yes, I agree parents do contribute to whether or not their child acts out, but it is my belief that they are not the sole cause of a child or youth resorting to violence as a means of coping or survival.

It is interesting to note that much of the literature and research about school violence suggests that most of the reasons for the conflicts in school have not really changed over the years. The problem is that now students solve them in different ways. This speaks to the fact that youths are not being given good problem-solving strategies, are not taught how to communicate effectively, and are unable to deal with interpersonal issues with any level of success. It has become increasingly evident that youth are now choosing guns and bombs as their premeditated method to resolve conflicts and are sense-lessly attacking multiple victims at random to express their anger, frustration, and revenge.

Robert Zagar highlighted the risk factors associated with violence back in 1991, but found that rarely, if ever, does one single factor cause problem behavior. It is the accumulation of experiences and influences that account for the positive or negative direction of a person's behavior. The more the youth accumulates these negative experiences, Zagar notes, the greater the odds of risk factors playing a role in possible use of violence to solve personal issues.

The following risk factors *double* the probability that a youth will commit a crime: (a) the family has a history of criminal violence, (b) the youth has a history of being abused, (c) the youth belongs to a gang, and (d) the youth abuses drugs and alcohol.

The odds *triple* when the above factors are combined with the following: (a) the youth uses a weapon, (b) the youth has been arrested, (c) the youth has a neurological problem that impairs thinking and feeling, and (d) the youth has difficulties in school and has a poor attendance record.

When investigating family violence and the link it has to violent behaviors in youth, one must understand that human behavior is a product of both genetic/biological and environmental factors. It seems that a combination of these factors creates a rich environment in the mind of the potential school shooter or youth who will act out. Many parents who have difficult children have had difficult childhoods of their own. It may appear that many of them parent by instinct and not necessarily by educated skills.

Many of these parents have not seen good parenting techniques modeled. They have learned to be resilient because life has taught them how to survive. Unfortunately, they have not been able to teach resilience to their children. They have not been able to teach their children the ability to bounce back from negative experiences, trauma, injury, stress, or threats.

It is true that some children are naturally hardy and possess positive, effective coping skills; these are not the ones who come to school with a gun to shoot people. The youth who will act is much more likely to be highly sensitive and vulnerable to experiences that cause fear or injury. These children have very little ability to process what is going on, and since there is usually no available adult to explain the situation to them, they create their own perceptions and understandings around these negative experiences. They tend to cope ineffectively with aggression and/or depression. They will internalize the experience and store the knowledge they have gained and use it to guide their decisions and actions at a future date.

It has been argued by many researchers that a baby's temperament can influence and predict with some level of accuracy whether a child will become a youth who acts out. Temperament is defined as those individual differences that show how we deal with emotions, attention, and stress; how we problem-solve; and how we self-regulate our emotions.

Children are born with a temperament style: (a) easy babies who adapt to routines and new experiences, (b) slow-to-warm babies who have a tendency to be more withdrawn, low-key, slow to react, display negative moods, and adjust slowly to new experiences, and (c) difficult babies who are irritable, react intensely and negatively to most experiences, are slow to adjust to new routines, and have major difficulty with change. Researchers indicate that a significant relationship exists between aggressive and violent behavior and childhood temperament. A difficult temperament has been linked to school failure and delinquency, attention deficit disorder, and oppositional defiant disorder, which are all associated with school-related violence.

Environmental factors interact with the child's temperament. Parents' childrearing styles influence the child's development. Parenting behavior creates the family climate, which in turn influences the extent to which the child will develop social skills, self-control, and the ability to comply with rules during adolescence. There are three types of parenting styles: (a) authoritative, (b) authoritarian, and (c) permissive. Each one of these styles creates a different child.

The most effective style is the authoritative parent who establishes clear and reasonable rules, makes reasonable demands, and consistently enforces and explains the rules. Authoritative parents are connected to their child in a responsive and emotional way. They encourage their children to make decisions, express themselves, problem-solve, and communicate effectively when there is a disagreement. These parents are more likely to teach social skills, self-control, limit setting, and boundaries. The results are a well-balanced adolescent who has skills to communicate his angst and emotions. This youth is not likely to act out in a violent way. However, there are exceptions.

The authoritarian parent sets too many rules without explanation and demands obedience and respect through coercive methods such as yelling, commanding, and criticizing. They often will punish more frequently but inconsistently and often the punishment does not match the offense. They may overreact with the punishment as a way of gaining and maintaining control. Little do they know that when they act in this way their control is very short-lived.

These parents rarely allow their children to make decisions and when a child does, it is usually the wrong one, leading to more conflict. The adolescent's opinions are not sought out and often are silenced. The results of this type of parenting lends itself to an adolescent becoming withdrawn, unable to make good decisions, usually making the wrong choices, and incapable of using coping skills to solve their situations. They become at risk for violent behavior due to anger and revenge. The seed is now planted for future acting-out behavior.

The permissive parent is one who makes few demands for obedience or respect and sets few if any rules. These parents are warm but overindulgent and tend to reinforce the child's coercive and manipulative behavior instead of prosocial behavior. Their adolescents are often encouraged to problem-solve and make decisions, but they offer little guidance or direction. They usually state that whatever the child decides is okay.

Adolescents raised by this type of parent have poor impulse control, defy authority, and are at a higher risk for anti-social and aggressive behaviors. These adolescents seem to develop a sense of entitlement. They are often selfish, egotistical, and make many demands. They become the spoiled brat who thinks that they can do whatever they please. Since they are impulsive they often will act without much thought or planning to their violent acts. They act on the spur of the moment and are contrite afterwards. Their behaviors are often repeated.

Connections are needed in families. Loving relationships are part of a family dynamic. Many children who act out do not have a close emotional attachment to another person within this family grouping. Connections are needed between adult and child to ensure good psychological development. If this connection or bonding does not occur in the early years, the child often will have problems with relationships and commitment.

The child will feel abandoned, rejected, unloved, withdrawn, and depressed. Once these feelings have taken root within the personality, an emotional numbing occurs, which is characterized by a loss of the capacity to feel anything for others. They externalize their pain by feeling victimized, threatened, and powerless, which in turn starts to manifest itself in violent actions. It is easy for the youth to disconnect from others. Once he has disconnected it is much easier to hurt someone because it will be the victim's fault for getting in the way. If the victim had not made the youth angry, he would not have hurt the victim.

Parental abandonment and disconnection play a huge factor in the risk factor of potential violent action behavior. The rates of disintegrated childhood disorder and reactive attachment disorder in the last ten years have skyrocketed. Is it a coincidence that rates of acting-out behavior have increased as well? There is a correlation and more research needs to be done to qualify that finding. A child who is abandoned or left with other family members believes he or she is not worthy. She or he suffers the loss of a caring adult and therefore feels unprotected, which leads to a belief that she is not good enough for the parent to stay and provide a secure and safe environment.

The child will not respect the parent and will look to other adults or powerful influences—often negative—to gain this sense of safety and security. If a child fails to find these connections, he begins to lack hope, is not future-oriented, has no purpose, and life has no meaning, which in turns makes it so much easier to shoot people and then shoot himself. No one will care if he is around or not—they never have. "Why not kill myself? I will not be missed," is the recording playing in the mind of this young person.

Another factor that contributes to the possibility of a youth acting out in a violent way is parents' lack of involvement in their child's life. Parents who do not show interest in the child's interests are more likely to not to be present for their child. This poor monitoring of the youth's activities and whereabouts will encourage secrecy between adult and youth. The youth will become more silent about these activities. He will leave without warning and disappear for hours and even days at a time. Parents will have no clue as to what and where their child is. This lack of ongoing supervision and monitoring creates uninformed parents.

The level of education of the parents and their socioeconomic status will greatly influence how they respond to their child's behavior. Uneducated parents tend to have poor parenting skills and a poor repertoire of skills in their toolbox of strategies to deal with these difficult behaviors. They are more likely to overreact or underreact. Either reaction is ineffective at controlling and guiding this type of youth. Lower socioeconomic status influences the availability of basic needs and resources.

Oftentimes money troubles are a source of problems and difficulty between the adults, which is transferred to the dynamics of the family. Youths need money that the parents do not have. Conflict arises, tempers flare up, and the adolescent is out the door. He is headed to school or the street and trouble will find this angry adolescent. Parents of higher socioeconomic levels also have issues with their adolescents, but those problems seem to manifest themselves in substance abuse and mild acting-out behaviors.

If a parent is a substance abuser or has a history of criminality, the odds for a troubled youth rise dramatically. Parents who are alcoholics, drug addicts, or involved in petty crime are often struggling to survive and feed their own addictions. Little time is left for the child, who is the witness to this addiction.

Two things occur in this situation: either the child takes the responsibility of the home and looks after himself and his siblings or he becomes resentful and lashes out at the impaired parent. Conflict is easily sparked in this environment, where one member is often abused physically or harmed in some way.

The youth begins to spend more and more time away from home and becomes involved with external groups (gangs) or is isolated within his own world. Either way, the emotional dysfunction is high due to the lack of a competent parent. The youth is unable to seek guidance from this kind of parent, so he will formulate his own solutions to problems. Chances are that the options he chooses will involve some level of violence, as that is all he knows.

All families function in some level of dysfunction. The level of dysfunction varies from moderate to severe dysfunction.

The moderately dysfunctional family often portrays a certain image to the outside world. Its problems are hidden below the surface and hidden from the community.

The at-risk youth who is acting out is forcing the issue by letting the community know that the family has secrets and is not perfect. One of the positives of this type of family is that the parents have skills, usually a comfortable income, and are competent in dealing with basic aspects of life. In the family that is severely dysfunctional, one or more adults may exhibit many at-risk behaviors and maybe functioning at a lower level than their children. If the youth is higher functioning than the parent, this differentiation in functioning limits the extent to which positive conflict resolution and problem solving can occur.

This type of family also lives in denial, has parental conflict, and has serious mental health issues and possible disability of some kind. The problems that at-risk youths have and the problems their parents have may differ, but the end goal of these separate behaviors typically runs parallel. These parents usually have difficulty processing their conflicts, and the situation is likely to deteriorate into communication problems. And these problems just transfer to the parent-child relationship.

Secrets develop and the child is now able to be manipulative, playing one adult against another. The youth wins because he is able to see that the parents are not on the same page around rules and expectations, so he exploits the situation. He becomes deceitful and manipulative to the point that parents lose control. As family functioning begins to deteriorate, the youth will begin to demonstrate increasingly maladaptive behaviors and move toward violence as a coping mechanism.

Parentification of children begins in early childhood in this situation; the parent starts to give responsibilities and privileges to younger children that would be better suited for older children or adults. These youth dictate the mood of the entire family by their strategies to maintain control. They become the disciplinarian and parents refrain from using effective techniques out of fear of causing more dysfunction.

These youth make decisions and hold the power of the family; parents give up the right to guide the youth from potentially dangerous situations. The youths learn by discovery what works and what doesn't, since the parents are of no use in helping them.

A history of physical, sexual, and psychological abuse plays a role in the family dysfunction that creates at-risk youth. Abuse is about power and control. Youths who resort to violence have power and control as their foundation of behavior. A youth who has been abused has suffered violence, pain, and chaos. The impact of these responses leads to coping mechanisms of denial, psychological numbing, self-hypnosis, dissociation, and extreme shifts between rage and passivity.

The youths who externalize their behaviors often become bullies and aggressive, while those who internalize their emotions become time bombs. They learn to negotiate the pain by themselves. They will withdraw and often show signs of depression, hyper-vigilance, and regression in behavior. Over-compliance may become a way to camouflage their emotions and their true intentions. They may dissociate, self-mutilate, and become suicidal. Increased drug use is prevalent.

Those who externalize often become hostile, provocative, and violent. They may kill or torture animals, destroy property through fire setting, and engage in explicit sexualized behaviors. Depending on the length and type of abuse, psychiatric symptoms may appear that have long-lasting effects. If this should occur, the youth has lost the ability to be rational and has an impaired vision and understanding of the people and environments around her or him. Paranoid symptoms may develop, leading to bizarre behaviors.

It is important to note that most children who have been abused do not become perpetrators of violent acts. Those who do become perpetrators are more asocial than antisocial. Their inability to form successful relationships with peers may be at the foundation of why they choose to target their peers in a violent shooting spree. Their feelings of low self-esteem and inadequacy fuel their need to be recognized and respected. They will make sure that people remember and notice them, and if pulling the trigger is the only way, they have nothing to lose.

Approaches to Prevention: Family Protective Factors

What is needed to help a youth at risk within the family situation? Not all programs and strategies will work for all parents and all families, but below you will find a variety of ideas to begin the discussion around intervention.

The first intervention is to build connections within the family. How do family members value one another? How do they communicate? How much time do they spend together in activity? Is there a time for the family to be home together? The child must be nurtured early on with loving affection and attention. He must feel valued and important. He needs to make a difference in his family.

A small amount of time devoted to the child's interests may build a connection that leads to a strong emotional bond. The adult and child need to be involved with adults outside the family. This provides a different role model for the child. It shows that there are different ways to solve problems. It teaches the child to communicate his feelings in a variety of ways. If by chance the parent is unable to provide nurturance, the child will have other adults to turn to for support and attention.

The way a family communicates and solves problems is a key indicator to the dynamics of the family. The youth needs to have a forum and a clear manner to express her opinions and express her views around certain issues. This ability to discuss problems with parents will indicate whether the youth feels heard and valued. The ability to problem-solve with a responsible adult will often provide parameters for the adolescent. These parameters can then be used to gauge future decisions and choice-making.

How parents view their son or daughter is important to him or her. If perceived parental expectations about school and performance are high and the youth believes that his parents are genuinely interested in his success, have reasonable expectations, and are supportive of his choices, this helps keep the youth from acting out.

Lack of continued parental interest is a trigger for many youths. Ongoing parental involvement and interest through presence, questioning, or discussion go a long way toward convincing the youth that he is supported. He believes that his parents do care.

Families who play together, stay together. Frequent shared activities between parent and child leads to building of memories, traditions, and relationships. The simple act of sharing an activity between two people builds a bond that later can be counted upon to diffuse difficult situations. Time is the key. The activity is not as important as the time.

Sharing of time is probably the one thing that most children desire. When a person shares time they are saying that because time is precious the child is precious and therefore important, which builds a sense of self-worth and self-esteem in the child. The consistent presence of a parent or adult when a child awakes, when a child arrives home from school, at the coming together for an evening meal to share the day, going to bed at night, and in all sorts of social activities leads to children who are emotionally healthy. Lack of these simple parenting elements often leads to acting out of violent behavior.

When working with dysfunctional families there are three forms of prevention: primary prevention (law), secondary prevention (support group), and tertiary prevention (community resources and support). When a youth becomes at risk, there are often many interventions for the individual, but the entire family is in need of attention as well.

It is important to remember the at-risk youth's behaviors are merely symptoms of family dysfunction. The behaviors often will escalate or decrease depending on the dynamics of the family. Any individual counseling can be a secondary or tertiary intervention. Individual counseling is often recommended over family counseling when the relationship between the parents is questionable, parenting skills are nonexistent, one parent is an alcoholic, or the parents are frequently absent from the home.

The involvement of the family in assessment, diagnosis, and treatment planning is essential if the parents have the capacity to participate and are not severely dysfunctional. Parents often should be offered personal counseling to help them deal with their frustration and build coping and problem-solving skills. Within the counseling, parents can be taught how to communicate with their children, learn different parenting approaches, and how to work as a team in their relationship and interactions with their child.

It is important that realistic and achievable goals be set within the counseling relationship so that parents can begin feeling successful in their attempts to deal effectively with their troubled child. It is much more about giving and teaching skills than it is about solving all the issues. Parents who have better communication skills do better with their troubled children.

A powerful prevention activity is parent education support groups. These can be developed by the school and/or community. An effective program is called STEP (Systematic Training for Effective Parenting). This program provides practical ideas for parents of children who are all at different stages of childhood and adolescence. There is a curriculum and lesson plans that guide the group.

Parent monitoring has also shown to be highly effective in helping parents deal with their at-risk youth. Monitoring has been proven to substantially reduce acting-out behaviors. Parents are taught how to ask their child where she is going when she goes out. Parents obtain a list of telephone numbers of their child's friends and call parents of their child's friends.

Parents also visit their child's school. The goal is to help the adult monitor and understand the circles within which their child interacts and to which she belongs. The fact that the parent is involved is often enough to curb some potential troublesome situations. An ounce of prevention goes a long way.

Educating the general public about the variation in family structures and individual differences will help increase awareness about different family dynamics and the challenges they present. Many local institutions such as hospitals, churches, and other community organizations can provide support for the various family structures like blended families, single-parent families, interracial families, and dual-career families.

A networking system can be created that provides the support and care needed for families in crisis. Investment from the community in these at-risk youth will have long-lasting effects, since youths are less likely to target the community if they feel part of it. Communities with a network of services such as runaway shelters, crisis intervention teams, support groups, hospitals, and outpatient services can provide support for the troubled youth or the family in need. Either way, both win and get the help they need. The at-risk family is a very special entity and needs a tremendous amount of attention to keep it functioning without tragedy.

6

Suicide: I Kill, Then I Die

Suicide is the process of ending one's life. It is common for school shooters to commit suicide after their acts of violence. The reasons, the motivation, and the patterns will be the topic of this chapter. There is a myth that suicide is due to mental illness, but most often the person doing the shooting is very calculated and organized around the actual act of shooting his peers and himself.

Nearly a million people commit suicide per year worldwide. There are nearly ten to twenty million suicide attempts per year. Approximately thirty thousand people kill themselves here in the United States annually and suicide is the third leading cause of death for teens between ages ten and twenty-four. There has been a 300 percent increase from 1950 to 1990, but the good news is that there has been a 35 percent decrease in rates since 2003.

Firearms are the most common means by which school shooters end their lives. This may be related to access, since many shooters have the gun right there and are able to turn it on themselves immediately upon completion of their mission. One must remember it is a mission; it is executed most often after long periods of planning and organization. Very rarely is it spontaneous; it can take years before the shooter actually acts on his thoughts. For some it may only be months if they have reached their boiling point due to harassment or anger. The tolerance for each individual shooter is varied.

If a school shooter is a white male (non-Hispanic) he is more likely to commit suicide after his actions. African Americans and Hispanics rarely use suicide as an option. Those who have completed violent crimes are more likely to survive the attack and will be imprisoned. It is common to see the white shooter move to final solution.

Mental health professionals have attempted to create a profile of an individual that may be at risk for suicide by creating a risk assessment inventory listed below. If an individual has several of these risk factors he is more likely to commit suicide after his actions.

1. Male
2. Age younger than 19
3. Depression (significantly clinically depressed)
4. Previous suicide attempts
5. Has had previous mental health interventions
6. Excessive alcohol and/or drug use
7. Rational thinking is lost or impaired
8. Ending of some sort of significant relationship
9. Has developed a plan for suicide
10. Little or no social support
11. Talking about suicide
12. Preoccupation with death
13. Taking unnecessary risks or exhibiting self-destructive behaviors
14. Out-of-character behavior
15. Loss of interest in things previously enjoyed
16. Setting affairs in place
17. Saying goodbye either in person or through a letter

The way a youth decides to commit suicide is unique to the individual, and trying to predict whether a person will commit an act of violence is difficult. It would be wonderful if we could take a look at a youth and predict with a certain level of accuracy whether he would become a shooter who ends up committing suicide, but there are too many variables and unknowns. There are common threads in the backgrounds of individual shooters that may predict the likeliness of becoming a shooter who commits suicide, but there is no foolproof way of determining this with any level of accuracy.

If we are to understand the adolescent or the youth who will be committing a school shooting, we need to enter his frame of mind. The first part of the analysis is to see what he is thinking and why. This addresses the motivation. If we look back at previous school shootings we see a few common patterns.

Youths who have been bullied, isolated, harassed, threatened, and made to feel secondary have been the majority of the shooters. Their commonality of experience is quite well defined. They were victims and unable to free themselves from victimization. There was no way out but to fight back and show others that they were someone in life. Several of the shooters have wanted to become famous, and what has happened is that they have become infamous.

They are seen as monsters full of hate and anger—the crazy guy who lost it and had to use violence to be noticed. The media plays a powerful role in portraying these youths as crazy, deranged, and out of it, because how else could anyone explain the actions? No one in their right mind goes out and deliberately shoots kids in school. The shooting is often about vengeance and revenge. It is a way for the shooter to assert and to be noticed.

Very rarely will the individual do it only to gain attention. Once the plan has been put into place, the shooter is organized and determined about the way it will be executed, and the final outcomes. He can predict with 100 percent accuracy that he will not survive the attack. He knows ahead of time that he will die. He knows that this is the only solution—the only way. He sees no other options.

If one analyzes the psychology around the thinking patterns of the shooter, one can understand that there is a systematic sequence of events that occur in the brain from planning to execution. First the shooter begins to have thoughts and fantasies about getting revenge on his tormentors. At what point it moves from fantasy to actual planning is uncertain. It may be after repeated tormenting or abuse from other youths or there is a trigger that occurs in the youth's life around a situation or a stressor.

One might believe that there is a catalyst for the beginning of the planning stages. The moment a youth makes the decision to shoot up his school or his peers is the moment the planning becomes real. He begins to scout out locations and observe routines and patterns of the school system. He begins to understand and record these observations and formulate his plan.

He becomes aware of the security measures or lack thereof in the school he attends. He begins to record the schedules of when students are in class and which class and in what area large groups of students congregate, like the cafeteria or the gym. He begins to track his potential victims if his anger is focused on specific individuals. If his hate is focused on the school system, then any place and any person is fair game.

This type of shooting is probably the most difficult to predict as it can happen anywhere, at any time. Schools are not prepared for this kind of attack. It is like a terrorist attack, and the element of surprise is the shooter's best tactic to making it successful.

Prior to most school shooting incidents, others know about the attacker's intentions and/or specific plans. Why the code of silence? If the shooter does tell others, why are the threats not taken seriously? Is it because people discount the fact that someone could actually go through with it? Is this the fatal mistake? It would be interesting to know how many plans for school shootings were known prior to the event. Most attackers engage in some form of behavior prior to the incident that causes concerns or indicates a need for help. Why are these indicators not noticed or addressed? Strange behavior needs to be addressed by either parents or school officials. However, it is to the shooter's benefit not to be too obvious or the plan will fail.

Once the individual has marked out the territory, he is better able to figure out what he needs to do. In this way he can arrive and deliver his destruction without any chance of being stopped. If a school happens to have security measures in place, he will figure out how to circumvent those measures and get his weapons of choice into the building. Some shooters only bring weapons to the site the day of the shooting, while others bring weapons on dry runs and see if they can sneak it into the school. If a shooter is successful at this, he may store back-up artillery in his locker in case of need.

The plan has started to become a reality in his mind. He has scoped out the school, routines are recorded, security measures are identified and planned for, and the planning of the attack begins—the how and the when. Most school shootings occur on weekdays, mostly Tuesdays, Wednesdays and Thursdays. It is almost deliberate that the shootings occur on these days. It is as if shooters want to give their peers a few days off school since they know that classes will be cancelled over several days because of the shooting. It may also be related to the youth reaching his boiling point because of an added incident, more bullying, or a failing grade that triggers his going home and getting ready for the next school day.

The fuse has been lit. The student has been pushed to the breaking point. He has reached the limits of his tolerance. It is time for action. He knows in his heart and mind that he will not survive this. He knows he must commit suicide. He is aware that he will bring shame to his family and that he will be forever hated by all in his school and town. He knows that living in this community will be hell for the rest of his life and that jail is a horrible place. He suspects he will be mistreated and abused even more if he ends up in jail; he will become the victim again. He will be a victim his entire life.

It is at this point that the decision to kill involves many levels of cognitive structures. He knows that killing is wrong, provided he has had some moral development in his childhood years. He is able to comprehend the results of his actions and he knows that there is no way out if he chooses to follow through with the shootings. It is my belief that once the decision has been made, there is a calm that occurs in the brain. The calmness of the decision helps create a bridge to the action of killing. He now is better able to rationalize his actions. It makes perfect sense to him; this is the only thing to do. Overall, is it the only right thing to do! All that is left to do is to decide when. The plan goes into action.

The day the attack is to occur, the youth awakens knowing that today will be the day he makes history. A history-making action will take place once he enters the school. He knows that he is doing the right thing, that he has no other options. If there were other options he would have thought of them, and since none have come up this is the only way. If he is going to target individual teachers or students he already knows where they are at that time of the day.

He knows that he must enter and shoot. There is no time for talking. In fact, many of the shooters do not speak at all. Very rarely will they ever engage in conversation with any of their potential or predetermined victims. Since most shooters are not marksmen, they randomly start shooting everyone they see. Bullets fly all over a classroom or designated area. Some shooters seek out their predetermined victims to make sure that they are truly dead, while others just randomly shoot all that are present.

If the youth does not have any predetermined victims, he will enter the school and just open fire. It does not matter to him who he kills. Sometimes victims are just in the wrong place at the wrong time. He shoots blindly into the crowd, so many more people are injured or killed. The randomness of the shooting and the bullets ends up killing many more people. Examples of this are Columbine, Virginia Tech, and Northern Illinois University.

The shooting is in full force. The shooter looks out into the crowd but really sees no one. He is blinded by his own actions. He does not take any satisfaction in his actions and is emotionally blunted. He sees the results of his actions, the chaos he has created, the running, screaming, the dead bodies, yet he continues shooting till all are gone or there is no more movement.

The calm has arrived, the calm he knew would come. He prepares to turn the gun on himself, which he has planned. He has practiced on how to hold the gun. He knows where the best place is to place the gun before he shoots himself. He has done the research and knows he will be successful. The outcome is planned and executed with a sense of finesse and style. He positions the gun, usually at the head or heart, and pulls the trigger. He is now at peace.

It is sad to see that almost all school shootings end with the shooter committing suicide. He will not be alive to tell why he did what he did. American society wants answers. We want to know why an individual would go through with such a horrible action. Unfortunately, we have not been able to get many answers from these young men. There have been insistences of some of them leaving letters or videos to explain their actions, but many do not choose to give an explanation. It is up to us to surmise what the motivation was.

Those who have left letters or videos indicate a series of common themes. They were all unfairly treated by someone, have felt hopeless or helpless to change their course in life, and have felt isolated and unloved. The need for acceptance by someone is a key motivator. When there is no one in your life who supports or accepts you, then where is the motivation to live and care about your life?

We as human beings need to feel connected and loved. The absence of love and acceptance is the common denominator in these letters. Lack of connectivity motivates the individual not to care about others, making it easier to kill them. It is much easier to kill someone to whom you have no emotional connection. It is like disposing of unwanted garbage in that young person's mind. If no one cares about you, why should you care about them? The decision to commit suicide is one that is not taken lightly on the part of the shooter; rather, it is considered the only way.

The tragedy is that these shooters ruin so many lives through the expression of their own rage and anger. It is not clear in retrospect whether their actions could have been prevented. The sad part in many of these stories is that help was needed and society could not provide the needed help until there a violent or illegal act was committed. These stories of school shootings are a wake-up call in that we as a society, school, and community must do better in assisting youths whose actions indicate they may be on a path to violent or destructive behaviors.

Suicide is an ending, the ending of a young life. Society still sees this act as one of shame and desperation. It highlights that people are weak and could not make it, and it denigrates individuals who do not have the proper coping skills to stick it out. Parents and teachers must examine their practices of dealing with their children or students.

Are you, the adult, creating so much helplessness and hopelessness that a child will want to take his life as the only solution to solving the situation that you are putting him in or inflicting upon him? The solution to preventing suicide in the young is to change adult behaviors and teach our children and adolescents that no matter what the situation or crisis is, there will always be an adult, an answer, or a way to deal with the problem. No problem is worth ending a life over.

7

School Crisis Prevention and Intervention

Crisis is part of life. It happens to good people and in great places. No one is immune from the effects and impact of crisis. Crisis develops over a period of time; it is rarely instantaneous. It may seem like it comes out of nowhere, but that is a myth. Crisis is a series of events that builds to a crescendo of actions. It seems that every crisis situation leads to learning and hopefully changes.

The 9/11 tragedy has led to major changes in economic, social, and international policies and procedures. Crisis prevention is a team, not a solo, effort. One individual can begin actions toward change, but it requires systemic change to prevent another crisis from occurring at the same magnitude as some of the ones that preceded it.

School shootings are a perfect example of this: with each situation comes new learning and interventions. In the last decade there has been a proliferation of manuals to guide school personnel in intervening in school crises. Legislators have required school districts to take preventative and remedial measures to address school crises.

Many scholarly experts have formulated a variety of definitions for a school crisis. There are three factors that seem to be common to all: disruption of the normal school routine, some level of emotional and psychological upset, and a need for plans, procedures, or protocols beyond what the school has in place at the time.

Situations have a way of being felt and responded to in a variety of ways. Depending on prior events, some schools are better prepared to go into action when a crisis occurs; for others the crisis collapses the whole structure and system of the school. Crisis may evoke fear, helplessness, shock, and/or horror in one population, while in another these emotions are present but not to the same degree of intensity.

Specific crisis preparation and preparedness strategists recommend developing a comprehensive crisis management plan, forming a multidisciplinary crisis response team, and using crisis drills. Research supports the effectiveness of the first two, and crisis drills for children have been found to improve skill performance and reduce fears. However, there is not much research to support the effectiveness of these drills over time.

The U.S. Department of Education has formulated a model of school crisis prevention and intervention. The model is divided into four parts:

1. Prevention: Awareness, assessment, mitigation, education.
2. Preparation: Planning, training, crisis communication plan.
3. Response: Immediate actions to restore security and safety.
4. Recovery: Postvention, crisis team support, postincident analysis and evaluation, revision of policies, refresher training.

The overview and specifics of each one of these steps are clearly presented in this document. The following discussion will only touch briefly on each area. Prevention is key. Educators must become more aware of what the risks are to life and school and they need to be on alert as they gather and filter information daily from a variety of sources within their buildings or complexes.

To be more proactive, they must document what they see and hear or what they do not see and hear, what is happening or not happening, and where their sources of information are. Is the information accurate? Are faculty and students aware of the underlying factors and issues within a school or within a social group and/or within an individual? Are people paying attention? What kinds of information is the surveillance producing? Is it accurate? Information and intelligence-gathering is ongoing at all times. Do the faculty and support personnel in the buildings, buses, cafeteria, and/or playground have their antennae out?

The next crucial step is how this information is treated. How is it interpreted? Are the sources credible? Are there biases toward certain individuals or groups within the building? Is the issue only within the four walls of the building or does it extend out to the community? Is the reported issue coming into the school due to social factors from the community? The assessment of risk is crucial in this information process.

The information needs to produce specific information about who is at risk. What are the warning signs? What is the time factor before the crisis—is it immediate? How extensive or serious is the risk? The team must be very focused in finding specific evidence to answer these questions. Does the assessment require immediate action, like increased supervision or surveillance or a call to law enforcement? The challenge is to be thorough and accurate.

The goal of any crisis preparation is to know what to do with the information and be ready. It requires the school and educators to self-assess their own process by asking several questions: Do we have the authority to respond to this particular crisis? What are we allowed to do? How do we mobilize internal and external resources? Who are our contacts? How accessible are the emergency responders? What is our system for communication within the school during the crisis? How do we respond in order to restore safety and security? What do we say and do for our students, staff, and parents? Hopefully these questions and self-assessment will lead to revisions in policies and procedures, or create new ones that will lead to crisis prevention. Once these policies have been created, better crisis communication will hopefully develop and the risks and reactions will be minimized.

In 2003, the U.S. Department of Homeland Security cited many recommendations to protect schools and soft targets such as hospitals, schools, malls, and restaurants, which are all vulnerable because people have access to them freely. The recommendations are:

1. Encourage personnel to notice and to report unattended packages and to not handle these objects.
2. Encourage personnel to know emergency exits and stairwells.
3. Increase security personnel.
4. Increase roving security personnel at varying times and routes.
5. Inspect restrooms frequently.
6. Inspect deliveries prior to any event.
7. Limit the number of access points.
8. Deploy visible security cameras and motion sensors.
9. Review crisis procedures, reaction protocols, how to handle threats, evacuation procedures, and alert notification procedures.
10. Conduct internal training exercises.

Obviously a school may do all the following and still be a target. The key is being prepared to respond in a way that is effective, efficient, and that leads to minimal injury or death. Obstacles include being unaware of the risk and denial or refusal to act on information. It is of utmost importance that the team collaborates to plan and that it uses the documentation received as an outline to plan intervention.

Crisis preparation depends on solid leadership from school districts, schools, and community agencies. Specific well-rehearsed protocols and procedures must be in place in anticipation of a crisis. Schools need to talk about the "what ifs." What if a stranger comes into the school with a gun? What if a student gets into a fight and comes back with a gun? Is the school ready?

Crisis response must restore physical and psychological safety to all as soon as possible. If a school shooting has occurred, how will the children and parents be reunited? Where are the emergency responders? What are they attending to? Are they able to reach the victims and injured? Is their safety compromised if they enter the building?

Rapid decisions may need to be made under highly stressful conditions. Who is taking the lead? Who has the authority to make decisions? If a school has a standardized decision-making and communication system and protocols and checklists, the people responsible can do their job and do it well. These established protocols could eliminate the need for discussions and guesswork. Established protocols may include lockdown, evacuation, and relocation. Each one of these protocols must be rehearsed and all members of the faculty must be well-trained in following set procedures.

Crisis recovery is a much more reflective time. This is when the system addresses the psychological, physical, and social impact of the crisis as well as the needs of those who have survived the crisis. The major questions here are how to restore the facility, how to help people psychologically to feel safe, and how to address the reminders and anniversaries of the crisis.

The gathering of support personnel, psychologists, counselors, teachers, nurses, and so on, is paramount to helping both children and adults recover from a traumatic experience.

Meetings, support groups, and memorials are all ways to help individuals deal with the crisis. Time does heal, but each person does have his or her own rate of healing. It is worth mentioning that no one can do everything, but everyone can do something. This mantra may empower people to do what they can with whatever skill they have to offer.

The Goals of Crisis Planning in School Shootings

Educators are very aware that they cannot predict and account for all possible scenarios. All they can do is be better prepared and respond in a more effective and systematic way to minimize the damage or trauma. It is the responsibility of school personnel to develop effective policies and plans for preventing a crisis. The specific goals of crisis planning are to create policies and procedures that:

1. Reestablish the safety and welfare of all within the school community;
2. Reunite students with families as soon as it is safe to do so;
3. Keep the community informed;
4. Return the school to normalcy and established routines;
5. Provide psychological support for those affected;
6. Have a system of referral for those students at risk for acting out;
7. Eliminate the ongoing threat to individuals at the school;
8. Maintain an effective crisis response team;
9. Use other postincidents as a guide. (Adapted from Kerr, 2009)

The conversations must occur prior to a crisis. Educators must have policies and procedures in place, and these must be kept current and active at all times. Districts must set their priorities for drafting policies that address any and all possible situations that could occur. The Internet has become a wonderful source of information for any type of data on juvenile behaviors, arrests, incidents, and violence. Districts can learn vicariously by looking at the many examples across this country. The discussion that ensues from this gathering of data may lead to a comprehensive crisis plan that addresses many crisis situations.

Mary Kerr created a mnemonic device to help crisis team members recall the essential steps in any crisis: BE CALM.

BE: Before you act, be sure you get the facts.
C: Call for help, communicate the instructions, and collaborate with other responder agencies.
A: Anticipate what could happen next and adjust the plan accordingly.
L: Listen to your audience and learn what it needs.
M: Manage the crisis, maintain the responders, and modify the plan afterward, based on what you learned.

This process, as she explains, is calming in that it provides a specific structure of action. It clearly articulates what people are expected to do at that time. It provides guidelines to shape thinking and reactions. All staff members are responsible for safeguarding the health and safety of students. All staff members are expected to exercise sound professional judgment, err on the side of caution, and show sensitivity throughout any crisis situation. It is with ongoing training that educators will be better able to respond.

School Shooting Crisis Response Procedures

The following list of procedures is meant as a guide only and is general in nature. Each situation will be slightly different and will require some adjustment to the order or type of procedure followed at a specific time.

1. The individual who learns of the threat or sees the individual with the weapon will follow established protocols for informing administrators or authorities. If time is crucial, an individual teacher or student calls 911 immediately. Crisis team is notified immediately.
2. The administrator will contact local agencies by calling 911 and will inform remaining school faculty of lockdown procedure or evacuation protocols. Contact district office and inform superintendent.
3. Staff members will move all other students out of the immediate area, and, if possible, students are to be locked into classrooms or areas away from windows or from the scene.
4. No staff member is to engage or disarm the shooter.
5. Administrator or designee is to provide emergency responders with detailed maps or charts of the school area and the area being affected.
6. School officials are to follow the orders of the police or S.W.A.T. team.
7. Administrator is to contact parents or guardians for information that may be useful to the emergency responders.
8. If the student is currently in counseling or receiving psychological help, the administrator will attempt to reach and inform the treatment provider of what is going on and get the provider's perspective on the profile of the shooter.
9. Do not give out details to the media as the situation is occurring as this may create panic and also fuel the ego of the shooter, who may want to have some level of notoriety and attention.
10. Hopefully, there is a peaceful resolution to the situation with no lives lost or major injuries. If injuries or deaths oc-

cur, the following steps will need to be followed after the immediate crisis is over:

a. Announce a meeting of the crisis team to plan how to deal with the deaths or injuries.
b. Support personnel team will need to be brought in for the general school population.
c. Do not do an assembly to gather students all in one place at this time.
d. Do not announce the deaths over a public address system.
e. Meet with your district personnel to plan actions to see if classes or preplanned activities will be cancelled and for how long.
f. Discuss how normal routines can be reestablished and the best way to do that.
g. Discuss how the students and community will express their emotions and reactions to the deaths. Memorial services must be the result of careful planning by a team of educators and mental health professionals. There should not be any rush to do this. The length of time before a memorial service will be variable, based on the individual situations of the shooting.
h. Anticipate any possibilities of copycat behavior and address this immediately with further evaluation and mental health counseling services.
i. Plan a debriefing time for all those involved in the postvention, including faculty, staff, crisis team, and any other members involved; they need support and time to process as well.

The business of crisis management is not only for school shootings; it involves all possible crises, including violent events, suicide, serious injuries, natural disasters, fire, bomb threats, terrorism, hostage-taking, kidnapping, and any threatening event occurring during school activities and/or involving members of the school community. Preparation for schools to respond to crises includes partnerships with other community agencies as appropriate (health and mental health service agencies, public health agencies, religious organizations, social service organizations, emergency medical services, fire departments, police, etc.).

Families and community agencies play a role and therefore must be clearly knowledgeable of the protocols. They must be able to articulate what is expected of them in a crisis situation. Do all know the protocols to be followed? Do they know where the safest parts of the school building are? Can they all identify the personnel responsible for decision-making and coordinating the response to a crisis? Adequate training of school personnel and practice must occur to see if all are able to follow the prescribed procedures and do them with a level of expertise and mastery. Only with practice will faculty and staff be prepared to make split-second decisions. There are no second chances in these life-and-death situations.

The National Education Association has detailed instructions on how to develop a variety of strategies for crisis management. It has developed an Internet-accessible toolkit that guides schools on preventive measures, interventions, and staff training. Detailed instructions are provided for telephone trees (for staff notification), preparation of staff lists identifying staff trained in cardiopulmonary resuscitation and first aid, identification of makeshift reunion areas, prepared badges or orange jackets that enable students to identify key personnel, checklists for school preparedness, planning for orderly release of students, and dealing with the media.

They also address the potentially disturbing physical reminders that might remain at school when students return after a crisis, curricula for the first day back to school, and memorials. All of this wonderful and useful information is available at the National Education Association's website, www .nea.org/index.html.

The prevention strategy most frequently used by schools is the crisis response team. The team is the hallmark of successful crisis management. The team is instrumental in developing preventive education programs, such as anger management/social skills, conflict resolution, and violence prevention. The team is on the front line and able to recognize that students at risk may need a variety of interventions. These may be psychological first aid and individual counseling, holding groups to help students process events, debriefing, and referring students for services.

Schools use crisis consultation with teachers as well, including providing general information about crises and referral information, and debriefing teachers. Providing information for teachers enables them to refer troubled students and is key to the prevention of another crisis. But who should be on the crisis team? What kind of individual is most effective? What kind of skill set is desired for this challenging role?

The personal and professional qualifications of effective crisis team members are something that must clearly be evaluated so as to have the most effective people in the right job at the time of the crisis. The following list states criteria for choosing specific people to be on the team. These criteria demand that the desired characteristics be found when choosing your team members. A crisis team member should be someone who:

1. Knows the community;
2. Is able to establish rapport quickly and meaningfully;
3. Possesses skills needed in a crisis, depending on the situation;
4. Has the capacity to accept direction and execute diverse functions under pressure;
5. Can multitask;
6. Is available at a moment's notice;
7. Is knowledgeable about the age group involved in the crisis;

8. Communicates clearly and sensitively under stress;
9. Can remain calm and efficient;
10. Is able to practice confidentiality to the utmost degree;
11. Is able to listen well;
12. Can use technology to access information;
13. Is very familiar with the school and the area within the school;
14. Can assume leadership if the leader is unavailable or injured;
15. Can work with existing security personnel to secure the school;
16. Has some medical or emergency training;
17. Has mental health training; and
18. Is proactive in problem solving rather than reactive.

It is definitely a challenge to find all these characteristics in one person. The formation of the team must include an assessment of who is on the team and what she or he can bring to the table in terms of skills. The goal is to find the individuals who have several characteristics so that they can jump in at any time in any role and be effective. These individuals work toward the resolution of the crisis and do not augment the level of crisis. The school team profile will include the principal, designee for backup, communications coordinator, maintenance staff, information site manager, relocation manager, school counselor, school nurse, staff notification coordinator, teachers, and staff.

The training of these individuals as a team must be given time and process to articulate what responsibilities are and how team members can effectively execute them in case of an emergency. It is highly recommended that the team develop a crisis response "go kit." The U.S. Department of Education has developed guidelines for school-level and classroom-level go kits. It is recommended that you check out the U.S. Department of Education Emergency Response and Crisis Management Technical Assistance center website at rems.ed.gov/

views/documents/HH_GoKits.pdf for examples as your school develops these procedures and kits when a crisis occurs. Examples of these have been provided in the help section later in this book.

Crisis Communications

We have all seen the mass hysteria as a crisis unfolds. We have seen countless individuals get injured because of panic and lack of information. How does a school prepare for effective communication? Do the school and school district have protocols to convey information and receive information from employees, students, families, and the general public before, during, and after a crisis?

The protocols must be clearly articulated prior to the crisis concerning what avenues will be followed and how these protocols will be executed during the crisis. The plan should include how schools plan to communicate with law enforcement agencies, emergency response agencies, and community members such as families. There has to be a plan for both the external audiences, such as those in the community, when they see or hear the media reports, and the internal audience, the teachers, parents, and students.

The psychology behind panic and hysteria is based on the formula developed by the U.S. Department of Health and Human Services' Substance Abuse and Mental Health Services Administration in 2002, which states that crisis plus heightened public emotions plus limited access to facts plus rumor, gossip, speculation, assumption, and inference equal an unstable information environment, which then leads to panic and impulsive acts and therefore more injuries or deaths.

The people responsible for handing out information need to be very clear about what their message will say, how it will be interpreted and listened to in terms of requests for specific protocols in specific actions. Make sure that the message is at the appropriate literacy level for the audience. You have to keep in mind what key messages you want your audience to hear.

What are the main points that will lead to calm and collectiveness? The sentences should be short and the word choice accurate and memorable so as to make a lasting impression in the audience. If there will be press releases, handouts, fact sheets, and/or letters, make sure that they have been checked and rechecked for accuracy. If a message is to be released to the press, what is the best way to do that? Are there alert systems developed by the school to contact all parents? It is also key to choose a spokesperson that will exude calm and confidence. This could be the principal, superintendent, or law enforcement official.

The way communication is handled during a crisis can prevent another crisis from occurring and may defuse the situation, leading to a positive outcome. Specific protocols for communication need to be developed for students, teachers, and parents. The goal is that the communication will maintain calm and keep all members accurately informed as much as possible so as to avoid hysteria.

In conclusion, when dealing with crisis intervention and prevention, one must be aware of how the school shooting will impact the community and its members. The schools and school districts must be diligent in responding to a crisis with specific protocols and procedures that people trust will work in keeping them safe.

The school districts must prevent critical incidents by becoming aware of the social and mental health factors influencing the populations in their schools. They need to get better at sharing information with all the stakeholders in their community. Districts need to become much more proactive in their early detection of impending incidents. Do the district and school administrators have heads-in-the-sand syndrome or do they truly have a handle of what the pulse is within the community?

It is important to assess and know with a level of accuracy whether or not the school district and school administrators can mobilize and facilitate the response to a school shooting. Is there an established crisis team with established protocols where everyone knows what to do at the moment of a school shooting? The administrators must be able to contain the crisis and prevent a spin-off crisis by maintaining responsible contact with all who are involved in solving the crisis.

Once the school shooting is over, can school officials maintain or restore the public's confidence in the school? A huge role for school officials will be how to support the families and friends of the victims of the school shooting. Officials will need to show sensitive outreach and compassion in how they hand out information and support to the community.

School officials will need to reexamine their protocols, procedures, and responses once the school community has returned to some level of normalcy. A school shooting evokes change in all who witness and participate. It is a life-altering moment. It is a moment that defines the past, present, and future.

8

Postvention: Supporting the School Community after a School Shooting

The crisis is over! Now what? Dealing with the aftermath of a crisis situation is a volatile situation, as there are many emotions flying around, ranging from rage and revenge to fear and shock to peace and tranquility. How does a school or an organization begin to do the necessary work to heal?

Postvention is a set of services provided to a school or community following a death of one or more individuals. The goals of postvention are to support those grieving the loss, to assist the school in returning to its normal routines, to identify and support those most at risk for severe reactions to the death, and, in the case of a death by suicide, to prevent contagion (Kerr, Brent, McKain & McCommons, 2006).

There is an established postvention process outlined next, but every tragedy has its own timetable. It is important to understand that there is not a clear recipe for postvention but there are several elements to consider when planning one. Each one of these elements needs to be clearly articulated and discussed fully before attempting to go into action. The teams involved in postvention must be prepared to take a look at how people are reacting to postvention strategies. It is essential to have a pulse on the school community and its members.

Key Questions in a Postvention Process

1. Have previous tragedies affected the school?
2. How has the school dealt with those losses?
3. How long were the victim (adult[s] or student[s]) at the school?
4. How well-known and well-liked were the victim(s)?
5. How much information about the death(s) has been reported in the media?
6. How many students witnessed the tragedy or death and what was their exposure?
7. How many students are thought to be at risk?
8. What are the ages of the students affected?
9. Do the victim(s) have other family members in the school district?
10. Is the school in session? (Kerr et al., 2006)

Each disaster has its own unique set of conditions and it is imperative that each school has a postvention coordinator that will take the lead in the process. This is not the time to figure out who will do what. Each school district needs to have identified individuals in each building who will take the lead immediately and will begin coordinating the process and postvention.

The following postvention implementation plan was developed by Kerr and associates. The information can be found in more detail in the *Postvention Standards Manual: A Guide for a School's Response in the Aftermath of a Sudden Death*. This manual is an excellent guide to help schools deal with tragedies around death and school shootings.

When a shooting occurs in a school and there are victims and injured, a plan goes into action as predetermined in earlier protocol meetings.

Step 1: Principal, superintendent, and postvention coordinator are all informed and mandated into the action plan.

Step 2: Coordinator gathers factual information, contacts coroner and law enforcement officials, and completes the identification of individuals and necessary paperwork as determined by the state.

Step 3: Coordinator contacts victim's family, provides condolences, supports family in making funeral arrangements, discusses with family how it wants the school involved in the funeral, and how the victim's belongings will be returned and/or handled.

Step 4: Coordinator organizes counselors for students and staff. Faculty is contacted through phone chain as soon as possible about the details.

Step 5: Coordinator approaches outside mental health agencies to provide ongoing support during the crisis. Mental health agencies provide support as per prior agreements or as pay-for-service as needed.

Step 6: Coordinator prepares with crisis response team an announcement to be read by faculty to the students in their classes. Principal prepares a letter for the parents. Coordinator locates all the victim's belongings and begins to remove names from any automated call lists. Coordinator confirms designated media spokesperson with the superintendent. Faculty is reminded to refer all questions from the media to the media spokesperson.

Step 7: Crisis team begins to compile a list of at-risk students to be individually screened. These could be those with mental health concerns, close friends of the victims, students presently getting help for drug or alcohol abuse, or individual classmates.

Step 8: Faculty meeting occurs before reopening of the school to discuss the following: facts of the shooting, funeral arrangements, an overview of the postvention services, procedures for dealing with distraught students, monitoring of grieving behaviors, policy on what do with gifts and memorials created at the school. At this time a letter will be distributed to be read to students. Faculty also will attend a meeting at the end of the day to debrief any issues.

Step 9: On the day of the funeral, school needs to be cancelled. Counselors need to be available postservice for debriefing students and families.

Step 10: Trained classroom teachers or counselors may need to conduct ongoing grief presentations and sessions for individuals or specific groups of students. Make sure that all students who are seen are monitored consistently and that there are follow-ups and check-ins over the months following the tragedy.

Step 11: Discuss the grieving process with faculty regularly. Remind faculty and staff to continue monitoring students and remind them that there is no time frame for grieving, that through natural supports, students and staff will get through these difficult times. Provide support to the community and parents as well through information sessions or workshops on dealing with a death or shooting.

Step 12: Coordinator meets with administrators and concerned parties to reevaluate the postvention process and procedures. The team plans for the anniversary date and special events. The team reviews student screenings and individual monitoring of those students. The team reevaluates the needs of the faculty and how best to support them to help support the students. Finally, the team makes recommendations to make the postvention more efficient and timely.

Post-traumatic Stress Disorder

Life is full of stress and activity. School shootings create a traumatic event for all who come in contact with it. Traumatic events are marked by a sense of horror, helplessness, serious injury, or death. Traumatic events affect the survivors of the victims who have been involved. Secondary impact can occur as well when seen on television.

Different people respond to trauma differently. Responses include feelings of fear, grief, and depression. Physical responses can occur like nausea, changes in eating and sleeping, and withdrawal from activities. For some it may last for weeks; others for months. There is no set pattern. Most people feel better within three months of the shooting, but if problems persist, the person may be suffering from post-traumatic stress disorder (PTSD).

PTSD is an intense physical and emotional response to thoughts and reminders of the event that last for many weeks or months after the traumatic event. The symptoms of PTSD fall into three broad types: reliving, avoidance, and increased arousal.

Symptoms of reliving can include flashbacks, nightmares, and extreme emotional and physical reactions to reminders of the event. Emotional reactions can include feeling guilty, extreme fear of harm, and numbing of emotions. Physical reactions can include uncontrollable shaking, chills or heart palpitations, and tension headaches (CDC, 2008).

Symptoms of avoidance include staying away from activities, places, thoughts, or feelings related to the trauma or feeling detached or estranged from others (CDC, 2008).

Symptoms of increased arousal include being overly alert or easily startled, difficult sleeping, irritability or outbursts of anger, and lack of concentration (CDC, 2008).

Other symptoms linked with PTSD include panic attacks, depression, suicidal thoughts and feelings, drug abuse, feelings of being estranged and isolated, and not being able to complete daily tasks.

Checklist: For Common Psychological and Emotional Reactions Following a Stressful Event like a School Shooting

The following is a guide for parents, school administrators, counselors, and teachers to monitor students in a post-crisis situation.

Characteristic	Present
1. Numbness	Yes/No
2. Mood swings	Yes/No
3. Feeling helpless	Yes/No
4. Sleep disturbances	Yes/No
5. Fatigue, low energy	Yes/No
6. Feeling overwhelmed	Yes/No
7. Sadness	Yes/No
8. Anger	Yes/No
9. Grief	Yes/No
10. Shock, feeling stunned	Yes/No
11. Fear that the event will recur	Yes/No
12. Startled response (jumpiness)	Yes/No
13. Nightmares	Yes/No
14. Self-blame	Yes/No
15. Self-depreciation	Yes/No
16. Fears	Yes/No
17. Uncertainties	Yes/No
18. Apprehension	Yes/No
19. Recurrent thoughts about the event	Yes/No
20. Depression	Yes/No
21. Irritability	Yes/No
22. Unhappiness	Yes/No
23. Difficulty talking about what happened	Yes/No
24. Wishing that the event never happened	Yes/No
25. Problems with memory or concentration	Yes/No
26. A sense of unreality about what happened	Yes/No
27. Reluctance to share feelings or talk	Yes/No
28. Hyper-arousal	Yes/No
29. Feeling keyed up, on edge	Yes/No
30. Muscle tension	Yes/No
31. Increased isolation or withdrawal from others	Yes/No
32. Increase in use of drugs or alcohol	Yes/No
33. Loss of interest in church or faith	Yes/No
34. Outbursts of anger, crying, or blaming others	Yes/No
35. Development of bodily symptoms	Yes/No
36. Headaches	Yes/No
37. Persistent colds	Yes/No
38. Chest pains	Yes/No
39. Delayed response to situation or event	Yes/No
40. Constant personal distress	Yes/No

Scoring:

1–10: Symptoms are a normal response to crisis.

10–25: Student needs opportunity for support from family, friends, and school counselor.

Above 25: A student needs professional mental health therapy to deal with PTSD.

In the postvention process it is imperative that some actions be taken within the first twenty-four to forty-eight hours of the school shooting. Students need to express their feelings and reactions about what happened to trained individuals who can explain to them what they are feeling and thinking. Students need to seek emotional support and comfort with trusted friends, family members, and colleagues.

Students will need to be taught that they have been through a traumatic event and that eventually life will return to normal. Teach the students how to limit their expectations about what they can accomplish in a day until the stress begins to diminish. Set up facilities to help them to relax, exercise, and engage in low-stress activities that demand little personal effort.

Help them understand the need to try and maintain a structured daily routine that includes a healthy diet and limits the use of alcohol and drugs. Help students identify their support systems: psychologists, counselors, pastors, mental health practitioners, parents, and friends.

Children respond to trauma in many ways and at different times in response to a crisis. Preschool children find it particularly hard to adjust to change and loss because they do not have the coping or communication skills to effectively voice their fears and concerns. Often we see a regression in behaviors, such as thumb-sucking, bedwetting, clinginess, and/or fear of strangers. Many children may experience pains and aches, disobedience, hyperactivity, speech difficulties, and aggressive or withdrawn behaviors (National Mental Health Information Center, n.d.).

Children in early childhood (five to eleven) may have many of the same reactions as above; they may withdraw from play groups and friends, compete more for the attention of adults, fear going to school, allow school performance to drop, become aggressive or find it hard to concentrate, and they may regress to early behaviors (National Mental Health Information Center, n.d.).

Adolescents (twelve to seventeen) are likely to have vague physical complaints, abandon chores and school work, withdraw, resist authority, become disruptive, or experiment with high-risk behaviors, and may experience guilt, feelings of helplessness, or deny their emotional reactions, (National Mental Health Information Center, n.d.).

The impact on learning for children and youth who have experienced a school shooting may be manifested in the following ways:

1. A decline in school performance.
2. Difficulty mastering new material.
3. Increased irritability.
4. Increased withdrawal.
5. Increased anxiety and depression.
6. Greater likelihood of engaging in risk-taking behaviors such as substance abuse, promiscuity, reckless driving, and suicide attempts (in adolescents).
7. Increased focus on the loss.

What Educators Can Do

1. Students can be offered additional supports, such as tutoring or participation in mentoring programs to assist them in maintaining their academic progress before academic failure occurs.
2. Listen to what students want to share. Listening is a powerful healing tool.

3. Protect students from becoming retraumatized. Sometimes other students may ridicule or bully other students who are highly emotional.
4. Connect with students about the loss and trauma, check in with them regularly, letting them know that you are available to them just to listen.
5. Model adult behavior that shows how responsible adults react to loss and respond in a crisis.
6. Teach about the normal signs and symptoms of grief and trauma so that students can assess and understand their own behaviors and learn new ways of coping.

There are several ways that the adults in schools and communities can help children and youths of the community deal with the crisis of a school shooting. It is important that adults answer questions about the event but not dwell on frightening details or allow the event to dominate and supersede any return to normal routines or activities.

The National Mental Health Information Center has provided the following list of tips for talking to children after a disaster. Some of these suggestions hold true for a school shooting as well.

1. Provide children with opportunities to talk about what they are seeing on television and to ask questions.
2. Don't be afraid to admit that you, the adult, can't answer all the questions.
3. Provide ongoing opportunities for children to talk. They will probably have more questions as time goes on.
4. Answer questions at a level children can understand.
5. Use this opportunity to establish a family emergency plan; feeling that there is something you can do may be very comforting to both children and adults.

6. Allow children to discuss other fears and concerns about unrelated issues.
7. Monitor children's television watching. Watch news reports as a family and discuss what is happening.
8. Help children express their emotions and recognize that a wide range of reactions is normal. Help children talk to teachers and other adults in their lives.
9. Try not to focus on blame.
10. Help children identify good things, such as heroic actions and assistance from officials and regular people in the community.
11. Consider family counseling if a child is experiencing many PTSD symptoms.
12. Family expectations may need to be adjusted for the child.
13. Teachers can work with family and help the child through art, play therapy, and encouraging group discussions in the classroom.

Guidelines for College Students

Virginia Tech and Northern Illinois University are both examples of how colleges and universities are vulnerable to school shootings. College is a time of self-discovery and exploration and should feel safe to those who attend a particular institution. No one can predict if a university will be a target; all one can do is be ready with a postvention protocol. School shootings assault college students' sense of safety in the world. The following is a list of possible interventions to consider after a shooting has occurred.

1. Keep your routine. Encourage students to do things that provide a sense of routine and predictability in their lives.

2. Encourage them to turn the television off. Watching news reports over and over affects the brain's capacity to process and store information. It also causes the student to relive the situation repeatedly. The events on television create images that may come back as nightmares or flashbacks.

3. Opportunities for youth to gather are crucial. These can be faith-based support groups, forums, or other student gatherings. The key is not to have all the answers but to bring them together. Allow students to have space to talk and know that someone is listening. The administrator of the college needs to listen as to what the fears are and how they might be addressed on the particular campus.

4. School administrators voice appreciation for students coming together. He or she makes a statement of observation, tries to normalize reactions, reinforces the value of community, helps students vocalize their fears and anxieties and understand that everything possible is being done to make them safe. He or she can discuss what services are ready to go into action, and where can students get guidance and support immediately.

5. School administrators need to resist the impulse to always have an answer for all situations. Voice the belief that the college as a whole will get through this situation together and that somehow individuals on the campus will cope and recover.

6. Entertainment and diversion are helpful. Having alternative activities is not bad; it gives a break from grieving that is not disrespectful and allows students to recharge their energies. It gives time to regenerate to continue coping.

7. Don't try to get students to talk about the shooting when they don't want to. The key is to consider how

questions are asked and facilitated. You have to help students feel safe about their answers and to ask clarifying questions. You want them to talk about their fears. Make sure to address their concerns about feeling vulnerable.

8. Don't rush the advice or try to take student's pain away. Let them process all the emotions.

9. Emotions are often overwhelming, so it is helpful to get students to stay more cognitive, which means focusing on what they think instead of what they feel part of the time. It is highly suggested that the individual working with the student helps him or her to seek out a variety of options to the problems, to effectively brainstorm possible solutions or explanations, and to redirect the youth to understand the connections between what he is feeling and thinking and how these thoughts and emotions influence his or her actions. It is essential to build self-awareness on the part of the youth.

10. Reassure students that all that can be done at this time is being done. Encourage students to keep their calm and not engage in any type of activity that may accentuate the situation or endanger further the people on campus.

11. Are the adults role models for the students? Students do as well as the adults around them. Is the school administrator voicing confidence in the safety of all individuals at the institution?

The final message is that school administrators must be competent and prepared individuals who have as a main goal the continued safety of all on campus. There are a variety of procedures discussed in earlier chapters concerning preventing school shootings or at least helping schools be better prepared to deal with them in an effective way.

Schoolwide Management in the Aftermath of Trauma

Trauma is different from grief. The needs of the student body and schoolwide management require specific considerations. The Crisis Management Institute in Oregon has formulated a list of schoolwide management strategies to help schools and universities cope with the aftermath of a crisis.

1. Group hysteria. Management of this issue depends on calm leadership and consistency in discipline. This is not the time to change behavioral expectations or make exceptions.
2. Rumor control. It is best to have one person answer all the questions and give out information. Discourage students from spreading rumors among themselves.
3. Model your belief that actions are being taken to return the school back to a normal routine. Inform students of the steps being taken to regain control by organizing physically observable activities that begin to address the aftermath. Students will then see that there is a sense of control in the building.
4. Students will not go back to learning until they feel safe in the school environment. They will need to have the opportunity to talk about their feelings and reactions, knowing that the event is not likely to recur, that the shooter has been caught or is dead, and that all students are completely safe.
5. Students need help to gain a sense of what is to come. School administrators need to refocus on predicting and preparing strategies. Do whatever is possible to give students and faculty a sense of what is to come and an understanding that routines are moving toward some closure or predictability.

6. Normalize for people the usual reactions to trauma. It is normal to have physical, emotional, and cognitive reactions to school shootings. Talking about these reactions helps people know that they are not going crazy.
7. Give students and staff opportunity to put words to their reactions and fears. This can be accomplished through individual and group sessions or debriefing held by professionals who can guide the process for traumatized individuals.
8. Do not have peer helpers or other student organizations involved in leading the discussions for students. All students need to be supported. The comprehension of these events is often beyond the cognitive ability or scope of skills of a student peer helper. Adults must remain in control.

These are just recommendations to help colleges and universities cope with the aftermath of a trauma. There are no easy or ready-made answers, only awareness that a plan must be put in place prior to any trauma. Hopefully these will never be used, but the college or university will be ready nonetheless.

Memorials

Memorials have sprung up over the years as a way to help the grieving express their emotions and have a place to go where they can feel a sense of community, comfort, and connectedness with others who are experiencing the same thing they are. Major memorials were set up when Princess Diana died in a car accident, after the 9/11 disaster in New York City, and at several of the school shooting sites.

Informal memorials are likely to spring up immediately after the shooting death of students or faculty. Plans to handle flowers, cards, stuffed toys, and so on, must be made in advance. Determine the time period that the memorial will remain in place: one week, two weeks, or a month?

Make sure to communicate to students in advance that the memorial will be removed after a specific time and indicate what will be done with the nonperishable items (e.g., stuffed toys). Providing alternate commemorative opportunities for students and engaging students early on in response efforts or an announcement about the family's wishes may help minimize spontaneous memorials.

Timing of memorial activities at school is another key component to consider. Commemorative activities and memorialization efforts should not be a focus of the crisis response in the immediate aftermath of a death. If done too soon, there may be a perception that the school is trying to close the chapter on grieving. Less formal but thoughtful commemorative activities developed over time with active student involvement are often much more meaningful and therapeutic to students and staff.

Postvention is all about responding after the fact. The most effective approach to preventing violence and protecting students is a balanced one that includes a variety of efforts addressing physical safety, educational practices, and programs that support the social, emotional, and behavioral needs of students.

Communication is critical in both prevention and postvention. Schools need to maintain close communication and trust with students and others in the community. Connectedness is what binds a school and community together. All members of that community need to be invested in the safety and security of the particular environment.

Support is critical for effective prevention and postvention. Educators must engage in comprehensive planning and coordination to prevent violence. Actions after the fact truly indicate whether a school district is ready and able to deal with a school shooting incident. The bottom line is that all parties (educators, parents, students, community people, and politicians) must work together, respecting each other's concerns and ideas, toward the common goal of keeping all children and all members of the school community safe from harm and trauma.

School Bereavement Reference List

Here are a list of possible articles dealing with student death and disasters. They are an excellent resource for stimulating discussion and/or professional development training.

Ayyash-Abdo, H. 2002. Childhood bereavement: What school psychologists need to know. *School Psychology International* 22 (4): 417–33.

Charkow, W. B. 1998. Inviting children to grieve. *Professional School Counseling* 2 (2): 117–22.

Doran, G., and N. D. Hansen. 2006. Constructions of Mexican American family and grief after the death of a child: An exploratory study. *Cultural Diversity and Ethnic Minority Psychology* 12 (2): 199–221.

Einsenbruch, M. 2004. Cross-cultural aspects of bereavement. II: ethnic and cultural variations in the development of bereavement practices. *Culture, Medicine and Psychiatry* 8 (4): 315–47.

Esmael, Y., H. Rubin, and S. Simon Shimshon. 2005. The meaning structures of Muslims, bereavement in Israel: Religious traditions, mourning practices, and human experience. *Death Studies* 29 (6): 495–518.

Gingerich, B. S. 2008. Ethnic variations in dying, death and grief. *Home Health Care Management & Practice* 20 (2): 205–7.

Hedayat, K. 2006. When the spirit leaves: Childhood death, grieving and bereavement in Islam. *Journal of Palliative Medicine* 9 (6): 1282–91.

Holland, J. 2003. Supporting schools with loss: "Lost for words" in Hull. *British Journal of Special Education* 30 (2), 76–78.

Jackson, K. 2003. Compassion fatigue: The heavy heart. *Social Work Today Magazine*, March 24: 20.

Lalande, K. M., and G. A. Bonanno. 2006. Culture and continuing bonds: A prospective comparison of bereavement in the United States and the People's Republic of China. *Death Studies* 30 (4): 303–24.

Lawhon, T. 2004. Teachers and schools can aid grieving students. *Education*, 124 (3): 8.

Lewis, M. L. 1998. Culture and loss: A project of self-reflection. *Journal of Nursing Education* 2: 398–400.

Neimeyer, R. A. 2002. Mourning and meaning. *American Behavioral Scientist* 46 (2): 2235–251.

Reid, J. K., and W. A. Dixon. 1999. Teacher attitudes on coping with grief in the public school classroom. *Psychology in the Schools* 36 (3): 219–29.

Weinstein, L. B. 2003. Bereaved Orthodox Jewish families and their community: A cross-cultural perspective. *Journal of Community Health Nursing* 20 (10): 233–43.

Winter, E. 2000. School bereavement. *Educational Leadership* 57 (6): 80–85.

9

Safe Schools

School is the gathering place of our future generations. It is a place students are mandated to attend until the age of sixteen. For many it is a place of wonder and learning. For others it is a place of hostility, fear, and violence. Violence has found its way into our classrooms. It cuts across all lines of culture and ethnicity and is not exclusive to any single group or class. It is reciprocal and communicable, contagious, and transmitted by overt, indiscriminant aggression, and in subtle, unintentional ways. Violence is not the human condition; rather, it is learned behavior that is preventable.

When studying violence it is important to understand that prevention of violence requires education of and by all segments of society. It requires a reassessment of how conflict is viewed and resolved. People have choices about how they behave. They are responsible for their actions and choices. The only way we will have safe schools is if school personnel understand the development of violence and the possible interventions at their disposal, and then become trained on the specifics of these interventions.

Violence is a societal problem that finds its way into the schools. Before we can begin to make schools safe, we need to reduce violence in our society. In 1994, James Kauffman put forth several ideas that might reduce the number of incidents of violence. He states that society should provide effective consequences for aggression. Does this mean building more prisons or teaching students how to behave in school?

We know that sending youths to prisons does not change their behaviors overall; in fact, many of them come out of prison and become lifelong criminals. Teaching youths how to have nonaggressive responses to problems is a better solution. Teaching specific self-control and problem-solving strategies will empower adolescents to be better able to deal with the challenges of school life. Early intervention is key to changing behaviors.

When children arrive at kindergarten and begin manifesting violent or aggressive behaviors, the school and the educators involved need to jumpstart the process of behavior modification, behavior support plans, and teaching new behaviors. It is crucial that the educators correct the conditions of everyday life in that classroom that foster aggression.

Educators need to document the frequency, duration, and intensity of the behaviors. They must find the function or source of the behavior and implement effective interventions to change the behaviors while the child is young. One does not begin to instill change in a fifteen-year-old student's behavior. Often it is too late by this time. Educators and schools need to offer more effective instruction and attractive educational options for kids in the school community. Children and youth will respond better to school-directed activities that give them a sense of belonging and acceptance.

Violence and aggression have no single cause or solution. If we are going to have safer schools we need to have a awareness and recognition that violence arises from multiple risk factors, including child abuse, school failure, family criminality, media violence, drug abuse, and other life factors. These multiple risk factors enter the school in the backpacks of the students. They bring their baggage and experiences with them. It is the school's responsibility to address and acknowledge these factors.

School safety encompasses several factors: (a) school climate, including individuals' perceptions about their school, its safety, and how they are treated by others; (b) school organization, policies, and rules; (c) environmental design of the school and campus, including how individuals use and move through spaces; (d) security measures, including interactions with potential perpetrators, surveillance equipment and personnel, locks, lighting, barriers, and alarms; (e) competent and timely threat assessment; (f) effective crisis responses to threatening situations.

The American Psychological Association developed several recommendations for reducing violence and keeping schools safe. They suggest that the education system teach all families and child care and health care providers how to deal with early childhood aggression via early childhood interventions in the form of extensive support services and training. In doing so, educators can provide developmentally appropriate school-based interventions in classroom management, problem-solving, and violence prevention!

If children are more aware of the factors that create problems for them and their school, there can be a promotion of and sensitivity to cultural diversity through community involvement in the development of violence-prevention efforts. Staff development training is essential in instructing and guiding educators on how to deal with violence on the school and individual level. All educators and personnel within a school are responsible for developing a positive school climate where all are valued and accepted. Schools that have developed a schoolwide discipline plan seem to be better able to promote and develop a positive school climate.

Many schools have decided that implementing school security measures such as mechanical forms of school security (videos, metal detectors, hand-held scanners, X-ray bag scanners, etc.) will keep the school safe from school shootings.

Some high schools have initiated random locker searches, personal body searches, and resource officers as a way to keep schools safe.

We have to be realistic: if an attacker wants to penetrate the campus's security system, he will. It is impossible to anticipate all the possible areas of threats. Many security systems need constant monitoring and many school districts do not have the resources or money to pay for these expensive security systems. For example, Columbine had a security video camera system, but no one was available to monitor the screens the day of the shootings.

The National School Safety Center has developed the following assessment tool to assist educators in evaluating their vulnerability to school climate problems.

1. Has your community crime rate increased over the past twelve months?
2. Are more than 15 percent of your work order repairs vandalism-related?
3. Do you have an open campus?
4. Has there been an emergence of an underground student newspaper?
5. Is your community transiency rate increasing?
6. Do you have an increasing presence of graffiti in your community?
7. Do you have an increased presence of gangs in your community?
8. Is your truancy rate increasing?
9. Are your suspension and expulsion rates increasing?
10. Have you had increased conflicts due to dress styles, food services, and types of music played at special events?
11. Do you have an increasing number of students on probation in your school?
12. Have you had isolated racial fights?

13. Have you reduced the number of extracurricular programs and sports at your school?
14. Has there been an increasing incidence of parents withdrawing students from your school because of fear?
15. Has your budget for professional development opportunities and in-service training for your staff been reduced or eliminated?
16. Are you discovering more weapons on your campus?
17. Do you have written screening and selection guidelines for new teachers and other youth-serving professionals who work in your school?
18. Are drugs easily available in or around your school?
19. Are more than 40 percent of your students bused to school?
20. Have you had a student demonstration or other signs of unrest within the past twelve months?

Scoring: Multiply each yes answer by 5.

0–20: Indicates no significant school-safety problems.

25–45: An emerging school-safety problem (plan should be developed).

50–70: Significant potential for school-safety problem (plan should be developed).

Over 70: School is a ticking time bomb (plan should be developed immediately).

An elevated score indicates a need to develop a comprehensive school safety plan. It would be beneficial to incorporate the community, law enforcement officials, and other concerned groups within the community. It is highly suggested that if your school scored highly you do an additional more comprehensive instrument called the School Safety Survey developed by Sprague and associates. This survey can further help in developing a safe school. A copy of this survey can be obtained from the Institute of Violence and Destructive Behavior at the University of Oregon.

Schools are vulnerable. They are places of learning, not federal maximum security prisons. Schools have a variety of factors that make them more likely to be targets. These factors are the design, use, and supervision of school space; the administrative and management practices of the school; the nature of the neighborhood; and the behavioral characteristics of the student population that attends the school.

If we compare unsafe schools with safe schools we find specific observable criteria. Unsafe schools lack cohesion; are chaotic, stressful, disorganized, and high risk; and have gang activity, violent incidents, and unclear behavioral and academic expectations. Safe schools are effective, accepting, free from potential physical and psychological harm, absent of violence, nurturing, caring, and protective. All schools can become safe with the right plan of action. We know what makes schools safe. We cannot be ignorant of these factors. We can evaluate a school and know with a certain level of certainty whether we have an environment ripe for violence or a school shooting.

If a school has a poor design and space, we need to invest resources into making it student-friendly and safe. In any assessment of a threat situation, it is important to do an accurate evaluation of any of the following to see if there is potential for a youth to enter or maneuver within the school environment. What are the heights of the windows? What are the number and types of entrances and exits? Where are the locations and designs of the bathrooms? What are the patterns of supervision by the adults in the building? What are the traffic patterns and their management by the faculty? What kinds of lighting are present? What is the ratio of supervising adults to students? What is the size of the school relative to the capacity?

If there is overcrowding, we need to look at alternative school year cycles or redistribution of student populations. If student alienation is occurring, we need to develop inclusionary values and practices throughout the school. We need to encourage and foster strong school bonding to the school environment and the school process. If there is poor supervision or limited involvement of faculty with students, we need to set clear and high performance expectations for all students and faculty.

High levels of student participation and parent involvement in schooling will build a sense of pride in the school community. If students are given an opportunity for skill acquisition and social development, they are more likely to respect the rules of the school. Students need to be given the opportunity to learn new schoolwide conflict resolution strategies to solve the minor and major conflicts of everyday school life.

In 1998 the U.S. Department of Labor produced a report called *The Appropriate and Effective Use of Security Technologies in U.S. Schools: A Guide for Schools and Law Enforcement Agencies*. Below you will find a list of their recommendations to keep yourself and your school safer from a school shooter or violent act.

1. Anticipate or imagine a threatening scenario and how you could handle it. Enlist the advice of others. Practice your strategy.
2. Plan your exit. Don't arrange your office furniture so that you can't get out quickly. Sit near the door if you can.
3. Don't advertise your whereabouts unnecessarily. Remove your name from your office door. Think twice about listing your name in a building directory; list the office instead. Paint over your name at a parking space.
4. Consider name tags for visitors and employees, body alarm buttons for some members, under-the-counter buzzers that alert security, two-way mirrors, security cameras, and controlled entry systems.

5. Require the school secretary to announce someone before letting them proceed into the building.
6. How will you communicate in an emergency: Phone? Fire alarm?
7. Schedule meetings with potential for trouble in high-traffic areas with security or multiple exits nearby.
8. In your office, do not have objects that can be used as a weapon. Don't have personal, home, or family information visible. Never serve hot beverages as they can be thrown in a moment of anger by an individual.
9. Be alert to your surroundings, parking lot, corridors, and school yard. Pay attention to people and what they are doing. Don't be caught off guard.
10. Learn how to de-escalate an agitated student or parent. Practice effective strategies such as honoring personal space, monitoring your body language and gestures, and using active listening.

These recommendations can be generalized to many settings other than schools and are often based on commonsense practices. It is crucial that school officials anticipate and plan for a school crisis. It is not feasible to think that it cannot happen in your school environment. It may be just a matter of time before something will happen. This list of recommendations helps you to assess your readiness, as well as to know that you have taken the necessary precautions to prevent a disaster.

A school needs to have a good threat assessment protocol to assess a verbal or nonverbal declaration of intent to harm another person. School administrators as well as other personnel need to have a shared knowledge and conceptual framework regarding school violence and threat assessment, which reduces the likelihood that personnel will engage in reactionary behaviors.

There has to be a multidisciplinary interagency team approach to ensure not only multiple perspectives and objectivity in evaluating threats but also to facilitate information sharing and actions necessitated by the conclusions. There has to be authority from the school board and superintendent's office to conduct interagency threat assessments. Administrators need to have an understanding of the relevant laws and regulations. Finally, training provides team members with the skills they require to conduct a threat assessment (Cornell et al., 2004).

It is of paramount importance that people within the school environment have the ability and know-how to effectively assess the situation and respond in a proactive way rather than a negative, reactive way, which may lead to more violence or deaths.

Schools can become more proactive by doing the following: (a) practice responding to different scenarios, do drills, lockdowns, and role plays to prepare both students and staff; (b) do not assume potential harm comes only from youth perpetrators—there are more adults who commit crimes than children or youths; (c) have a good crisis response plan that involves but does not rely solely on law enforcement—past shootings have indicated that school personnel responded first, with law enforcement arriving later; (d) use crisis communication codes that are straightforward and will be understood by those unfamiliar with the building; (e) spend time getting to know the communities that send students to your building as well as the neighborhood surrounding the building; (f) monitor websites where students may be posting information that could inform you about a threatening situation and advise the parents to do the same. The Internet is a great source of information, especially sites like MySpace and Facebook.

The nature of the neighborhood served by the school also plays a fundamental role in the assessment of school climate and safety. If there are high levels of crime to persons and property, drug and alcohol infractions, domestic violence, child abuse and neglect, and lack of cohesion in the community, these issues will enter the school.

If there is a high percentage of the student population that is eligible for free and reduced lunch because of poverty in the community, we can guess a substantial number of at-risk students are enrolled, there are many juvenile arrests or academic standards are not being met, and we will see many youths not invested in their school or education. In many of these situations, schools can play an important role in buffering or offsetting the impact of risk exposure through the development of social resiliency and essential skills, as well as through emotional and group support.

Leadership and management practices of the school are key components to the success of a good safe-school plan. An evaluation of the quality of the administration and their leadership skill and style is important in leading the school. Some leaders have practices that increase the vulnerability of the school to a school shooting or a violent incident.

The leader must promote and foster a positive, inclusive atmosphere where diversity is celebrated. They must have clear and consistent expectations around student supervision, recognition of students, and know-how to build relationships between faculty and students. They must have a plan for the direct teaching of social-behavioral, academic, and interpersonal skills. A leader must be collaborative and able to lead by example. He or she must be able to provide effective academic support for all students, regardless of issues, and support teachers in the following areas: classroom management, academic instruction, and meeting of educational standards.

Walker and Associates developed strategic approaches that can reduce the likelihood over time of a school tragedy. Their recommendations are to (a) secure the school, (b) address the peer culture and its problems, (c) involve parents in making the school safer, (d) create a positive, inclusive school climate and culture, and (e) develop a school safety and crisis prevention response plan. If a school wants to begin movement toward positive change, it must self-evaluate and see how it can integrate the following recommendations into its plan of action.

It is important in some schools to rebuild school culture to make schools safer. All members of a particular school community need to reexamine some of their beliefs around school violence and school shootings. The real horror is that young people die, not where they die. The majority of homicides occur in student homes or on the streets, not in school.

Some people still cling to the hope that schools can be made safer if we just install enough surveillance cameras and metal detectors. However, these instruments do not build or improve school culture. Safety comes from human relations. Schools can become safer if they are places where children and youths are valued, accepted, have a sense of belonging, and are nurtured to acquire skills that will make them better citizens.

Most kids already know how to listen, how to help, and how to assert themselves. The question is why they lack the dispositions to act in these ways. We need to make sure that all students have a place in the system called a school.

Throughout this country we have seen an increase in zero-tolerance policies as a way to prevent school violence or school shootings. One difficulty with zero tolerance is that it does not affect everyone equally. There seems to be a varying level of enforcement depending on who you are, where you come from, or what you look like. In reality, zero-tolerance policies put safety at risk. When students are punished they are more likely to strike back.

A safe school environment is one where students are able to really trust and be known and trusted by adults. Zero-tolerance policies do not help kids learn new behaviors by teaching them new specific skills. In some cases, where the zero-tolerance punishments are extremely harsh, the student becomes a criminal. If the situation had been dealt with in a more effective and proactive way, the student may have been able to regain some level of self-respect, and might not have gone out to get a weapon to deal with anger.

Some school officials who deal with youth misbehavior give a very specific message as to what happens when there is a violation of an expectation. If the school administrator calls the police and the youth is hauled off to juvenile justice system in handcuffs, the message is given very quickly to all within the school that you had better not make a mistake, and if you do, you are gone. How does that build school climate? In my opinion it does not. If kids with problems are seen as disposable commodities, how do we stop the cycle of violence?

It is my belief that we begin by identifying the deficits and strengths youths have, and provide them with the necessary supports and services that will allow them to grow as individuals who can acquire the necessary skills to make better choices when faced with problems or insurmountable issues and emotional upheaval.

Parents and communities can play a major role in developing safe schools. Educators need to create a parent advisory planning group at each school devoted to school safety issues for that school. People who live in the community have all kinds of information about the community and its special problems and strengths.

Educators can advocate for parents to teach their children adaptive, nonviolent methods of responding to bullying, teasing, and harassment at school and ways to avoid encouraging their children to strike or fight back. An antibullying program supported by both parents and educators will go a long way in changing school climate. Educators can help parents become more aware of how to secure weapons at home and of gun safety.

The National Rifle Association has published excellent guidelines for dealing with weapons. Educators can also make available for parents the best information on effective parenting practices, and provide access to training and support in more effective parenting to parents who seek it. Sometimes a little bit of information can have huge impact on the way parents deal with their children. Parents and schools need to become partners in the battle against school violence.

Effective schools are safer schools. There are many published research studies that have shown that a school climate that is positive, inclusive, and accepting is a key component of an effective and safer school. Common characteristics of both types of schools are that they create and promote a set of school-based positive values including civility, caring, and respect for the rights of others. Giving and teaching these skills is required; it is no longer acceptable to think that children and youth are learning these values in the home environment.

Effective schools also teach students how to separate from their own lives the exaggerated media images of interpersonal violence, disrespect, and incivility to which they are exposed daily. Children are bombarded by media images that are inappropriate. Educators must act as the reality check for children so that they can have some barometer to know what is acceptable and what is not.

Schools need to counter these images and messages with replacement messages of kindness, sharing, and respect. They need to teach children how to be respectful, responsible, and safe. Children need to have consistent schoolwide rules and behavioral expectations to stay grounded and retain a sense of direction as to what is expected in terms of behavior. By doing this, schools become places that are orderly, positive, well-managed, and safe.

10

Crisis and Corrective Teaching for Troubled Youths

All children need teaching in one form or another. Adults have many opportunities every day to foster learning in many ways. They have the responsibility to help children understand their feelings, thoughts, and actions. Children are faced with issues and problems every day and do their best to solve these issues with the information and skills they have learned or acquired through modeling.

Generally, children are pretty good at asking for guidance from the adults in their life. Unfortunately, aggressive and violent kids tend to deal with their problems, both familiar and unfamiliar, in ways that produce negative and harmful consequences for themselves and those around them. It is paramount that these youths receive specific guidance from their family or school.

Corrective teaching has been around for years as a way of helping these youths learn new behaviors. Corrective teaching as defined by the Boys Town program for at-risk youth is a process that caregivers use in response to a child's failure to do something he or she should do, or to correct a youth's misbehavior. Through corrective teaching, adults provide alternative responses for youth to examine when faced with the aggressive behavior or negative behaviors.

Corrective teaching consists of nine steps and is characterized by three central concepts: description, relationships, and consequence. Description is describing a behavior in words and actions, role-playing, and practice. The relationship concept involves using warmth and showing genuine concern for the youth. It is about building self-esteem in the youth. Consequences include feedback, losing a privilege, or a restitution that occurs. It is important that a balance and equilibrium be attained in all three areas.

The first step is initial praise and empathy. This begins the change in thinking patterns for the youth. The adult models acceptable praise and empathy for the child's situation. The adults thanks the youth for using more positive behaviors.

The second step is description/demonstration of inappropriate behavior. The adult gives very specific feedback around what was done or failed to be done. The description should be brief, spoken in a way that the child can understand, and followed by a demonstration of what the appropriate behavior should be or can be. It is important to teach rather than nag. One must spend the time in explanation followed by guidance on how to do it, and then praise the efforts.

The third step is consequences. One needs to be aware that punishment does not change behavior. If an adult is going to give a consequence, it must be something that is not aversive but shapes the thinking around the behavior. If something is taken away or imposed, the youth needs to know how it is related to his actions or behaviors. The best type of consequence seems to be when a youth earns negative points for misbehavior and positive points for appropriate behaviors. The student can earn back any lost points by practicing an alternative appropriate skill. This approach gives the youth hope.

The fourth step is description and demonstration of appropriate behavior. This is very straightforward, involving a simple and brief explanation of the skill or behavior the youth should use in place of the inappropriate behavior. It is explained in a way that allows the youth to understand what you expect of him or her. The link between the desired and undesired behavior is obvious and not ambiguous.

The fifth step is rationale. This is where adults take the time to explain to the youth what the benefits are of using the new behavior. The correlation of how the new behaviors benefit them personally, how they benefit others, and how they help them have more successful interactions becomes more obvious. This prevents the youth from thinking only of themselves and thinking more about how his behaviors and actions affect others. As a result the youth begins to learn and develop better morals and positive values.

The sixth step is the request for acknowledgment. The adults do a check-in with the youth to make sure he understands the rationale and what is being taught and what is expected of him in terms of new behaviors. It is crucial that the adults doing the teaching not move on to other steps before the youth completely understands the rationale.

The seventh step is practice. The youth is asked to practice the new skill or behavior in a role-playing situation. The child gets to practice it over and over again so that she can be successful. It helps to build confidence and help the youth know that if the situation happens in real life she has options.

The eighth step is feedback. The adults guide the youth through the practice of the new skill and help him fine-tune his new behavior. Youths can practice the skill, get feedback, and refine the action again to receive more feedback until it becomes an automatic response to the problem situation. Positive correction is a powerful incentive and motivator.

The ninth step is general praise. Adults praise a youth for her efforts to learn and practice a new behavior. This praise is ongoing and it helps the youth see that people are noticing and recording her efforts.

Many youths who act out violently have patterns of behaviors that are noticed early in their school lives. Corrective teaching is a strategy that can be used for youth as a preventive strategy. It provides them with the help that they may need to make better choices. Educators can provide this strategy through classroom teaching or one-on-one teaching with a school counselor or other support personnel. Corrective teaching—a process that enables adults to develop and strengthen relationships with kids—can become part of a child's behavior plan or individualized education plan. Relationships are often what are missing in the lives of the youth who does a school shooting.

Educators need to be aware of their own behaviors when dealing with a youth who is at risk of doing a school shooting or acting out in an aggressive way. Here are ten tips that may be used as a starting point to your intervening at the time of the crisis or prior to an incident.

10 Tips for Crisis Prevention

1. Be empathic.
   a. Try not to judge or discount the feelings of others.
   d. Whether or not you think the feelings are justified, those feelings are real to the other person.
   c. Pay attention to them.
2. Clarify messages.
   a. Listen for the student's real message.
   b. What are the feelings behind the facts?
   c. Ask reflective questions and use both silence and re-statements.
3. Respect personal space.
   a. Stand at least 1½ to 3 feet from an acting-out person.
   b. Invading personal space tends to increase the individual's anxiety and may lead to acting-out behavior.
4. Be aware of your body position.
   a. Standing eye-to-eye and toe-to-toe with a student sends a challenging message.

    b. Standing one leg-length away and at an angle off to the side is less likely to escalate the individual.
5. Ignore challenging questions.
    a. When a student challenges your authority or a facility policy, redirect the individual's attention to the issue at hand.
    b. Answering challenging questions often results in a power struggle.
6. Permit verbal venting when possible.
    a. Allow the student to release as much energy as possible by venting verbally.
    b. If this cannot be allowed, state directives and reasonable limits during lulls in the venting process.
7. Set and enforce reasonable limits.
    a. If a student becomes belligerent, defensive, or disruptive, state limits and directives clearly and concisely.
    b. When setting limits, offer choices and consequences to the acting-out individual.
8. Keep your nonverbal cues nonthreatening.
    a. The more a student loses control, the less that individual listens to your actual words.
    b. More attention is paid to your nonverbal communication.
    c. Be aware of your gestures, facial expressions, movements, and tone of voice.
9. Avoid overreacting.
    a. Remain calm, rational, and professional.
    b. Your response will directly affect the student's behavior.
10. Use physical techniques only as a last resort.
    a. Use the least restrictive method of intervention possible.
    b. Physical techniques should be used when individuals are a danger to themselves or others.
    c. Physical interventions should be used only by competent/trained staff.
    d. Any physical intervention may be dangerous.

By following the tips listed, you will have the best possible chance of providing for the care, welfare, safety, and security of everyone involved in a potential crisis situation. Crisis moments occur when students lose physical and rational control over their behavior. These crisis moments do not sprout into being without roots; there are almost always warning signs that let you know an individual's behavior is escalating. By using the tips discussed, you can often intervene before the crisis becomes dangerous.

Anger Cycle: The Pathway to Violence

Many youths who act out violently have issues around anger control. They do not have effective strategies to deal with the emotions that arise out of their inability to solve problems in an effective way. Usually it takes years to develop an anger problem. This problem is deeply rooted in frustration and lack of resolution of some life issues.

Hill Walker and Associates have been instrumental in identifying the anger cycle and its manifestations in youths. They have stated that there is a predictable cycle that all individuals go through when they become angry. They put forth the idea that when a stimulus occurs in a youth's life, he responds with a series of thoughts and feelings, which in turn leads to actions. Obviously, if there are any dysfunctions or cognitive distortions in this process, the youth is more likely to get angry. Eventually the cycle becomes part of the regular patterns of behavior.

The cycle of anger is formulated in seven steps: calm, triggers, agitated, acceleration, peak, de-escalation, and recovery. The speed at which the steps cycle through the individual's brain will depend on how many coping skills the individual has to deal with whatever is creating the problems that are leading to the anger.

There are identifiable behaviors at each stage.

Stage 1: Calm Stage

At this first stage the youth and child is able to demonstrate appropriate behaviors and is often productive and interacting in appropriate ways.

1. Exhibits on-task behavior.
2. Follows rules and expectations.
3. Is responsive to praise.
4. Initiates positive behavior.
5. Is goal-oriented.

Stage 2: Triggers Stage

At this second stage we see a variety of possible triggers that may set off the student in a variety of ways and settings. At times it is hard to know exactly what the triggers are unless we have prior knowledge of the behaviors or the behaviors have been observed in a series of events.

School-Based

1. Conflicts.
2. Changes in routines.
3. Provocations.
4. Pressures.
5. Ineffective problem solving.
6. Errors.
7. Corrections.

Non-School-Based

1. Ineffective home environments.
2. Health problems.
3. Nutritional problems.
4. Sleep deprivation.

5. Substance abuse.
6. Gangs.

Stage 3: Agitation

At the third stage of agitation we begin to see certain behaviors manifesting themselves as a response to the triggers.

Increases in Behavior

1. Darting eyes.
2. Nonconversational language.
3. Busy hands.
4. Moving in and out of groups.
5. Off-task, then on-task behavior.

Decreases in Behavior

1. Staring into space.
2. Subdued language.
3. Contained hands.
4. Withdrawal from groups.

Stage 4: Acceleration

At the fourth stage, we begin to observe the student ready for fight or flight. The student is noticeably distressed and is beginning to demonstrate certain behaviors that serve as indicators of future acting out or explosive-type behaviors.

1. Questioning and arguing.
2. Noncompliance and defiance.
3. Off-task behavior.
4. Provocation of others.
5. Compliance with inappropriate behaviors.
6. Criterion problems.

7. Whining and crying.
8. Avoidance and escape.
9. Threats and intimidation.
10. Verbal abuse.
11. Destruction of property.
12. Serious behavior in general.

Stage 5: Peak

The fifth stage is peak. If a youth reaches this level then the best thing is to get out of the way! He or she is no longer rational and trying to intervene is not wise or safe. It is at this stage that it is likeliest that a youth will lash out and become violent. The following behaviors are the results of reaching peak in the cycle:

1. Serious destruction of property.
2. Assault.
3. Self-abuse.
4. Severe tantrums.
5. Hyperventilation.

Stage 6: De-escalation

The sixth stage is de-escalation. The crisis is over and the youth is coming down from the explosive behavior. It is at this stage that adults need to be very aware not to retrigger the student by what they say or do. It is best to leave the child alone for a period of time. It is suggested that the adult read the child's responses and nonverbal cues to check in with him. Often the following responses are evidenced, so it is best to leave the youth alone till these behaviors disappear or become manageable.

1. Is confused and/or disoriented.
2. Attempts to withdraw.

3. Makes attempts at reconciliation.
4. Engages in denial.
5. Tries to blame others.
6. Is responsive to simple directions.
7. Is responsive to manipulative or mechanical tasks.
8. Tries to avoid discussion, except to blame others.

Stage 7: Recovery

The seventh and final stage is recovery. The situation has regained a certain level of control and calm. The student is back at pre-anger levels. She is more open to having the situation processed in a verbal way.

1. An eagerness for independent work or activity.
2. Subdued behavior in group work.
3. Subdued behavior in class discussions.
4. Defensive behavior.
5. An avoidance of debriefing. (Adapted from Muscott, 2006)

The important concern when dealing with angry youths and children is to know first what the main triggers are, how they are ignited, and how adult behavior fuels these triggers. It is imperative that adults working with troubled youth know these triggers inside out, but are also aware when the youth will more likely act out. Triggers become warning signs that will lead to a certain level of predictability.

It is very difficult to predict if a youth will bring a gun to school and shoot others, but there is no difficulty in determining youth who are angry. Their lack of positive coping skills is evident each time they lose control or act out. We know who the candidates are for angry outbursts; we just need to be more available earlier to change their behaviors.

One method for anger control was developed by John F. Taylor. He developed the ACE Method for Anger Control. The method's purpose is to teach children (fourth through twelfth grade) how to use anger in a constructive manner. Children will learn to: define anger, discover ways to express anger, correctly manage anger, and utilize cognitive anger management techniques.

To "win" the anger game, one will need a powerful ACE. Anger can be successfully channeled by taking action using ACE.

- A = *Adapt* to the situation.
- C = *Confront* the stressor.
- E = *Escape* from the stressing situation.

The strategy is further broken down in the following way: *Adapt* to the situation—making changes within oneself.

- First and foremost it is essential that the individual become aware of his or her anger patterns in order to be able to move toward the possibility of doing something different, hopefully more proactive than reactive when reacting to stressful events or people.
- Change what you are doing that might accidentally be making things worse.
- "I'm angry about failing the math test—maybe I could talk to the teacher about taking a retest tomorrow. I could study for it after school today."

Confront the stressor—talking to other people to get them to change how they are acting.

- "That bothers me; please stop it."

Escape from the stressor—leaving the situation as a display of firmness and determination not to continue being hurt or oppressed.

- Not to be confused with leaving the scene of conflict in order to cool off and calm down.

- Better to aim at *adapting* and *confronting* rather than *escaping*.
- Good to ask an adult (parent, teacher, counselor, etc.) about the decision to *escape* before taking action.
- "I tried to *adapt* and then I tried to *confront*, but I'm still feeling hurt by the way the other teammates are treating me, so I'm going to quit the team."

Once you have taught the youth or child the ACE method, it is key that you continue building the awareness of the child in terms of his own behavior. Teach children how to avoid mishandling their anger.

Don't be RUDE.

- R = Repeated useless venting.
- U = Underexpressing.
- D = Dumping.
- E = Exaggerating.

Each one of these letters stands for a specific identifiable behavior. Using the acronym may help build self-awareness for the youth who has problems with the behavior and anger control. The adult must take the time to highlight for the youth what each letter stands for and how the youth can change behavior through more awareness and understanding of what sets her off.

R = Repeated useless venting.

- Does not address the problem.
- Example: Running outside or pounding a pillow.

U = Underexpressing.

- Keeping anger inside and minimizing it.
- Can lead to anxiety and/or depression.
- Pent-up anger can explode.

D = Dumping.

- Misdirecting anger onto irrelevant targets.
- Example: Kicking the cat.

E = Exaggerating.

- Built-up anger from previous circumstances is discharged in current situations far beyond the level appropriate to the current stress.

The benefit of these methods is reframing the frustration of dealing with anger into a game that can be won. Children are empowered to utilize anger as a tool. The program can be adapted to fit a wide variety of situations and ages. Acronyms make it user-friendly.

Crisis Teaching

Crisis teaching is a strategy that many educators do not know how to implement because very few preservice teacher programs teach this type of instruction to their prospective teachers. Many educators are not prepared to deal with youths or children who have totally lost control and are manifesting dangerous or aggressive behaviors.

Crisis teaching is the art of teaching youth self-control strategies, that is, cognitive and behavioral techniques that empower youth to calm themselves when they become upset. By using self-control strategies, youth are able to stop their usual negative responses, think of alternative ways of coping, and choose better ways of dealing with their problems.

The goal is to help kids to look at their options, get their needs met in socially appropriate ways, stop and think how they can cope with stress and problems, and consider how they can achieve calmness and success in solving conflicts and

personal problems. The goal is to build a level of self-awareness in youth so that they can recognize when they need to
use a self-control strategy. Another goal is helping youth recognize triggers or anticipate events that will lead them to act
in negative and hostile ways.

It is highly encouraging for youth when they see the benefits of their efforts. They are better able to live by the rules,
make good decisions, and deal with others in a more positive
way. When working with troubled youth it is imperative that
teaching of self-control strategies occurs in noncrisis times. If
teaching is to be the most effective, it must not occur when a
youth is in crisis and/or negative behaviors are occurring. The
youth is more likely to listen and adapt to the new strategies
when he is better able to process what the strategy is trying to
help him with.

Here are some examples of self-control strategies:

1. *Deep breathing.* Take a deep breath through the nose,
   hold for two seconds, let out through mouth. Repeat
   two to three times. When calm, speak.
2. *Journaling or drawing.* Find a calm place, draw or write
   what you are feeling and thinking. When calm, show
   your work.
3. *Take time to cool down.* Find a quiet place, take an agreed
   time away. If more time is needed to calm down, ask for
   it calmly.
4. *Positive self-talk.* Use positive I-statements to calm yourself down. Example: "I can get myself under control."
   Repeat until calm.
5. *Muscle relaxation.* Clench and squeeze fists for five seconds, then release, roll neck in circles, scrunch shoul-
   ders, rotate ankles, raise eyebrows up and down,
   scrunch face and release.

It is key to use the right strategies for the right kid. The
strategy needs to help the student out of crisis mode. Some-

times there will be a trial-and-error period in discovering what will work and what won't. Crisis teaching is used to help the youth regain certain level of self-control.

Crisis teaching has three steps: phase 1, staying calm; phase 2, de-escalating behavior; and phase 3; cognitive strategies.

Phase 1, staying calm. The goal is to prevent extreme emotional outbursts and to get youths to recognize their behavior and put a stop to it as soon as possible. It is important that the adult dealing with the difficult youth also remain calm in her interactions. When an adult uses corrective teaching strategies it is essential that the instruction be guided in such a way as to build the possibility that youth will be able to make a statement of empathy. If the behavior continues, give statements of understanding, describe what was done wrong, and describe what to do right. Praise improvements in behavior and give reality statements. Offer the youth the opportunity to work through the problem with a positive correction statement. Hopefully she will become calm and the discussion or resolution of the issue can occur. If resolution does not occur, move on to phase 2.

Phase 2, de-escalating behavior. If the youth is still manifesting the inappropriate behaviors, the adult helps the youth choose one of the self-control strategies. If he does not, then the intervening adult chooses one. At this time the adult gives a statement of understanding, describes what was done wrong and describes what to do right, praises improvements in behavior, and gives reality statements. Test the youth's self-control with two simple instructions. Review with the youth the behaviors he should use that demonstrate self-control. If the youth is calm, move on to phase 3.

Phase 3, cognitive strategies. In this phase the teaching occurs to try to instill new cognitive strategies in patterns of behavior and thinking in the youth. The goal is to help the youth learn how to accept consequences or practices that come from making the choices he makes. At this phase, the goal is to rewire the thinking processes for the youth. The goal is to positively reinforce when the youth is demonstrating good self-control. The other goal is to teach accountability for his actions and reactions.

Crisis teaching is not meant be a rigid, all-or-nothing teaching tool. It provides guidelines for adults so that they are better able to meet the needs of the individual with whom they are working. Calming kids during a crisis and teaching self-control is an interactive process. As the adult you need to be aware of your own behaviors, especially if you are upset. It is hard to expect self-control from a child when you, the adult, are not calm. The goal is not to control children, but to teach them how to exercise self-control.

Reactive Aggression

Many youths who are involved in school shootings are individuals who manifest aggression externally. They tend to be bothered and frustrated by the actions and reactions of others. They generally are impulsive and react emotionally. When they become upset they have great difficulty controlling their aggressive behaviors. Those individuals who do not have good coping skills usually use aggression and thus harm their relationships or see no other option but to use violence to communicate their needs or frustrations. They do not possess the communication skills necessary for good resolution of problems.

Many school shooters have unhealthy and hurtful relationships with others. Those who act out against others are seen as bullies, while those on the receiving end of the bullying are seen as victims. The position of the school shooter is crucial in predicting the likeliness of him acting out aggressively. Many of these youths are not well-liked and have experienced a lot of criticism. They are extremely distrustful of others. Since many of these youths have severe relationship issues, it is imperative that they have significant adults in their life who will help them develop new, positive relationships.

It is vital that these adults use effective praise and encouragement to develop new behaviors. Many of these youths do not have the skills to respond positively, because for most of their life they have made bad choices or responded in destructive ways. So many of these youths do not look before they leap! As the significant adult in their life you want them to become aware of their thinking and the physiological signs being manifested by their thinking that precede aggressive behaviors.

Adults can set up kids for success by preparing them to deal with behaviors or situations that may set them off towards violent behaviors. As youth learn to better recognize all the signs of difficult situations, they can refer to their toolkit for strategies that will not lead them to taking a gun and shooting the sources of their frustrations or problems.

Many school shooters react aggressively because of distorted thinking. They inaccurately perceive cues from others or misread the intent of others. One must teach these individuals how to recognize their distortions and how to change their thinking so that they can assess situations more accurately and positively. Cognitive distortions come in many different levels and stages. Filtering is one of the most common distortions. In filtering, the youth dwells on a single negative detail of a situation, ignoring all other positive details or other types of information. This may be enough for obsessions to develop, which commences the contemplation of revenge and action.

At times these youths will use overgeneralization, where they base their conclusions about a situation on only one piece of information or one experience. Because they are unable to see all aspects of a situation, they become fixated on the person or institution who has done them wrong. It is as if tunnel vision develops.

There are two possible ways youths can distort their feelings of being in control. One way is believing that others control them totally, or they are totally responsible for others around them. The youth believes that everything is being done to him, so it is easy to be angry and resentful of those around him. He experiences feelings of helplessness and hopelessness. He believes he has lost control and no matter what he does, he can't get it back. This is the youth who gets the gun and comes to school with intentions to kill.

The fallacy of fairness is often at the root of acting behaviors. If there is a perception of unfairness, the youth develops feelings of resentment that may lead to a belief that others need to be punished or tested to make sure that fairness occurs. Several of the past school shooters have stated that they were treated unfairly by their peers or their school.

There are several strategies to help youth with cognitive distortions. Their goal is to help aggressive or disturbed youth find better ways to manifest their anger and frustration than to kill other people. The first step is to have the youth describe the situation or event that is causing difficulty. You help the youth look at external factors, considering the views of others and how the youth processes things internally. The next step is to help the youth identify his thoughts, particularly the ones he has before aggressive behavior. If there are distortions in perspective you help clarify the thoughts for him.

Once the distortion has been identified, the adult must teach the youth how to reframe the statements that are distorted. You help the youth to see situations from another person's perspective. The youth learns that others have feelings and that his behaviors affect him and others. An additional strategy is to teach thought-stopping. The youth envisions a stop sign, and whenever he gets a negative thought that may lead to a negative behavior he tells himself to stop and tries to replace the negative thought with an alternative positive thought. The goal is to teach self-awareness and self-monitoring.

Many youths with troubled lives in school may benefit from individual and group therapy. However, most studies have shown that counseling is not as effective as believed.

Many of the psychotherapeutic techniques tend to be relatively nonspecific, making it difficult to assess the effects of the treatment. Many school shooters do not reveal their intentions to school counselors in sessions. The relationship between therapist and youth may play a factor in whether or not the youth acts out. If it is a good one the youth is more likely to seek guidance and deal with his anger and frustrations in the therapeutic relationship as compared to manifesting it in an aggressive act.

Some school shooters have had pharmacotherapy as part of their backgrounds. For some, the shooting occurs after they have stopped taking their medications. Others may have needed the stimulants, antianxiety medications, or antidepressants, but were unable to get access to them if their behaviors were not recognized as needing medications. It is highly suggested that both pharmacology and nondrug therapies should be used in combination to treat aggressive youth. The importance of monitoring the youth and the medications is of great concern for all who interact with the youth.

In a review of many situations that involved school shootings, one common factor seemed to be present in all the backgrounds of the shooters: they all had difficulty with social skills. Many of them had severe deficits in this area. Some had never gotten appropriate social skills instruction at school or at home.

Social skills instruction needs to occur in a variety of levels of skill acquisition. It needs to be tailored in such a way that skills are scaffolds; one skill builds upon another. Each level must be demonstrated and mastered before the next one is attempted. The youth using the checklist must self-monitor and be able to recognize that she has mastered a particular skill. If an adult is creating the plan, there must be several instances and situations where the youth can learn and practice the skill. At times you may need to create the learning situation so that the student is able to acquire the skill. Role plays and real-life situations are the best ways to practice and master the skills. The following checklists have been adapted from the Boys Town Program for Aggressive Youth (Sterba & Davis, 1999).

Social Skills Checklist

Level 1 skills have been introduced and the youth is able to demonstrate them with some level of consistency and predictability. The youth is now able to show he has mastered these skills daily and in most circumstances or situations. The youth is ready for level 2.

Once the skills in level 2 have been demonstrated and mastered with consistency and the skills are becoming automatic, it is time to move on to level 3 and more advanced social skills.

This completes level 3. The youth now possesses a repertoire of social skills. If the student is ready and able, then it is time to move on to complex social skills that are required of healthy individuals.

This is the end of level 4. If you are able to accomplish the acquisition of these skills in a troubled youth, the chances are excellent he will never resort to using a gun to solve problems or deal with helplessness, victimization, or frustration.

Level 1:   Basic Social Skills

Skill	Demonstration	Mastery
Accepting consequences	Yes/No	Yes/No
Accepting criticism	Yes/No	Yes/No
Accepting "no" answers	Yes/No	Yes/No
Following instructions	Yes/No	Yes/No
Disagreeing appropriately	Yes/No	Yes/No
Talking to others	Yes/No	Yes/No

Level 2: Intermediate Skills

Skill	Demonstration	Mastery
Accepting compliments	Yes/No	Yes/No
Accepting decisions of authority	Yes/No	Yes/No
Anger control strategies	Yes/No	Yes/No
Asking for clarification	Yes/No	Yes/No
Asking for help	Yes/No	Yes/No
Correcting another person	Yes/No	Yes/No
Following rules	Yes/No	Yes/No
Getting another person's attention	Yes/No	Yes/No
Getting the teacher's attention	Yes/No	Yes/No
Ignoring distractions from others	Yes/No	Yes/No
Listening to others	Yes/No	Yes/No
Making a request	Yes/No	Yes/No
Making an apology	Yes/No	Yes/No
Positive self-statements	Yes/No	Yes/No
Peer reporting	Yes/No	Yes/No
Resisting peer pressure	Yes/No	Yes/No
Saying "no" assertively	Yes/No	Yes/No
Seeking positive attention	Yes/No	Yes/No
Structured problem-solving	Yes/No	Yes/No
Waiting your turn	Yes/No	Yes/No

In conclusion, it is important when working with youth who are socially inept, come from troubled lives and families, or have violent histories or developmental and psychological problems, that you reach out to them either personally or through support organizations. There will be times when the individual will not respond to your first attempts at intervention, but maintain that connection.

Continue reaching out nonstop. Your persistence may pay off and you will be able to reach this troubled youth in a way that will prevent him from acting out violently with peers or family. The youth needs to become your paramount concern if he exhibits behaviors that may give warning signs of using violence in the school or home.

Level 3: Advanced Skills

Skill	Demonstration	Mastery
Accepting defeat or loss	Yes/No	Yes/No
Analyzing skills for different situations	Yes/No	Yes/No
Analyzing social situations	Yes/No	Yes/No
Choosing appropriate friends	Yes/No	Yes/No
Controlling emotions	Yes/No	Yes/No
Cooperating with others	Yes/No	Yes/No
Coping with anger and aggression from others	Yes/No	Yes/No
Coping with change	Yes/No	Yes/No
Coping with conflict	Yes/No	Yes/No
Coping with sad feelings	Yes/No	Yes/No
Dealing with an accusation	Yes/No	Yes/No
Dealing with being left out	Yes/No	Yes/No
Dealing with contradictory message	Yes/No	Yes/No
Dealing with embarrassing situations	Yes/No	Yes/No
Dealing with failure	Yes/No	Yes/No
Dealing with fear	Yes/No	Yes/No
Dealing with frustration	Yes/No	Yes/No
Dealing with group pressure	Yes/No	Yes/No
Dealing with rejection	Yes/No	Yes/No
Decision-making	Yes/No	Yes/No
Delaying gratification	Yes/No	Yes/No
Expressing appropriate affection	Yes/No	Yes/No
Expressing feelings appropriately	Yes/No	Yes/No
Expressing pride in accomplishments	Yes/No	Yes/No
Making new friends	Yes/No	Yes/No
Making restitution	Yes/No	Yes/No
Negotiating with others	Yes/No	Yes/No
Persevering on tasks and projects	Yes/No	Yes/No
Preparing for a stressful conversation	Yes/No	Yes/No
Preventing trouble with others	Yes/No	Yes/No
Problem-solving disagreements	Yes/No	Yes/No
Relaxation strategies	Yes/No	Yes/No
Responding to complaints	Yes/No	Yes/No
Responding to others' feelings	Yes/No	Yes/No
Responding to teasing	Yes/No	Yes/No
Self-advocacy	Yes/No	Yes/No
Self-correcting own behaviors	Yes/No	Yes/No
Self-talk or instruction	Yes/No	Yes/No
Setting appropriate boundaries	Yes/No	Yes/No
Sharing attention with others	Yes/No	Yes/No
Spontaneous problem-solving	Yes/No	Yes/No
Sportsmanship	Yes/No	Yes/No
Use of appropriate language	Yes/No	Yes/No

Level 4: Complex Skills

Skill	Demonstration	Mastery
Accepting self	Yes/No	Yes/No
Altering one's environment	Yes/No	Yes/No
Asking for advice	Yes/No	Yes/No
Assertiveness	Yes/No	Yes/No
Assessing own abilities	Yes/No	Yes/No
Conflict resolution	Yes/No	Yes/No
Displaying appropriate control	Yes/No	Yes/No
Expressing grief	Yes/No	Yes/No
Formulating strategies	Yes/No	Yes/No
Gathering information	Yes/No	Yes/No
Goal setting	Yes/No	Yes/No
Identifying own feelings	Yes/No	Yes/No
Laughing at oneself	Yes/No	Yes/No
Maintaining relationships	Yes/No	Yes/No
Moral and spiritual decisions	Yes/No	Yes/No
Patience	Yes/No	Yes/No
Planning ahead	Yes/No	Yes/No
Rewarding yourself	Yes/No	Yes/No
Self-monitoring and reflection	Yes/No	Yes/No
Thought stopping	Yes/No	Yes/No

In protecting and helping this youth, you are also protecting many others, innocent people who do not deserve to be shot or killed by a child feeling hopeless and worthless. Only when all adults make a commitment to providing the highest quality care possible to all youths and children can we ensure a safe environment for all.

11

School Curriculum: Lessons for Preventing School Violence

People say that school is a place to learn, one that leads to great changes in the young and encourages them to become the best they can be. If that is the mission of education, then we can educate children and youth to show citizenship, peaceful behaviors, respect for diversity, and tolerance; we can educate for human dignity and foster positive attributes that will take children into the world and make them successful human beings.

If American children are to embrace equality and justice as core values and help transform their cities and communities and possibly the world, becoming more tolerant of others is not enough; youths and children also must come to see, analyze, and work against the structural and social practices that continually create and recreate a country of division, the "us versus them," the in-crowd and the out-crowd, the haves and have-nots. Children need to be taught that differences need to be celebrated if we are to discontinue a system of injustice and inequality. America is one nation with many Gods. How do students learn to accept the freedom that people have in this country to practice the faith of their choice?

Youth who have lashed out at other people often have targeted one group over another, popular kids, gay and lesbian kids, blacks or Latinos, Muslim students or groups, girls and/or women, gangs, or anyone they feel has targeted them or in some way humiliated or wronged them. Nationally, approximately 78 percent of principals reported having programs to address violence in their school (Kaufmann et al., 2000). Today in many of this country's schools you will find a wide array of violence intervention programs and services, including counseling, crisis intervention, skills training, peer programs for students, community programs, teacher programs, and security measures.

Under counseling services you will generally find victim assistance and support services, individual or family counseling, post-traumatic stress groups for observers or victims, services targeting ethnic, religious, or racial conflicts and child abuse education. However, often the student who needs these services does not get referred or identified early enough before the tragedy of the shooting.

Social workers and school counselors are excellent at teaching skills training. They use individual therapy to teach conflict management, social skills training, prosocial behavior curricula, skill streaming, groups for aggressive children, and leadership training. The school shooter is rarely identified early on for these groups or strategies because he may be flying under the radar of educators.

Many often are loners and do not generally cause external problems to their classmates. However, some have manifested a variety of acting-out behaviors that are and would be seen as warning flags. It is during one of these trainings that the educator may identify the root cause of the anger, frustration, or hopelessness and begin teaching skills to a potential school shooter. These skills can enrich his options and provide choices other than a gun to solve his problems.

Peer programs for students will often help foster positive peer culture in friendship clubs and afterschool sports clubs where a youth can, and hopefully will, find inclusion and acceptance. A word of caution: any type of peer program needs to be monitored carefully by adults. Many school shooters do not have a vested tie to the school because they feel that they are not wanted or valued.

Build inclusion and acceptance in a positive relationship and a youth is less likely to shoot you. It is easier to shoot an enemy or a stranger; there are no emotional ties or connections that may cause the youth to hesitate before pulling the trigger.

Community programs are alive and well in many small and large communities. They can take the form of antigang programs, services that address community violence, police antiviolence programs, parent support groups, church groups, and youth groups. The way children are involved and incorporated into their community builds a bridge to protecting and respecting the individuals within that community. If children are taught early on to respect where they live and go to school, they are less likely to come to the school and shoot members of that community.

Teacher-based programs are also known to be effective in changing behaviors. Teachers learn through training how to address violence in their classrooms. There are extensive programs that target classroom management, antibullying programs, and academic programs aimed at aggressors, victims, and observers. Teachers teaching students about how to solve problems and helping children become more aware of their own behaviors and actions will be preventive in nature. There is no way of knowing if a teacher teaching this type of program has prevented a school shooting, but the good news is that the phenomenon of school shootings is very limited.

Few evaluations have assessed the effectiveness of interventions normally used by schools, such as expulsion, suspension, referral to special education, detentions, mediation, and counseling. Some educators believe zero-tolerance gun laws to be the major cause of the overall decline of weapons on school campuses—many students who brought weapons to school were expelled immediately. My concern is, where do these students go once they have been expelled? Is it to wreak havoc on the community? Join gangs and come back and hurt nongang members or citizens in that particular community? Monitoring where expelled students go is crucial to the safety of the community and school.

In the work I do with school districts around children and youths with emotional behavior issues, I have developed a model program to help educators deal with frustration and programming for these students. The model is called AWARE: A-assess, W-what, A-ask, R-respond, E-evaluate. The purpose of the model is to assess, consult, and program for children who have violence issues. The model is circular as you can see in the diagram.

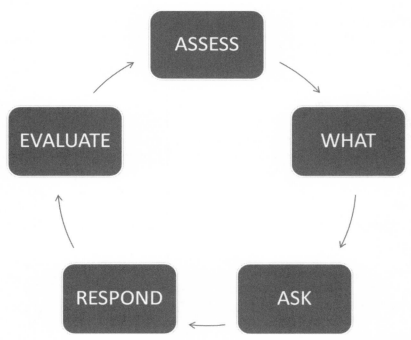

Figure 11.1.   AW.A.R.E. Model: Assessment Process for Evaluation of Behavioral Concerns in Childrens and Youth

Each section of the model is directly connected to what happens before and after the component. Each one of the sections builds upon information gathered. It is important that a document be kept throughout the process so that all evidence is clearly articulated in the right section and leads to the team making the correct decisions on the data provided. If insufficient data is present, the team must continue its investigation of the situation or problem behaviors.

Step 1: Assess the Situation

In this first step the team must assess what is going in the situation. Information is gathered about family influences, issues, traumas, history, and the details that go along with the profile, such as where and when the behaviors are occuring and the frequency, duration, and intensity of the behaviors.

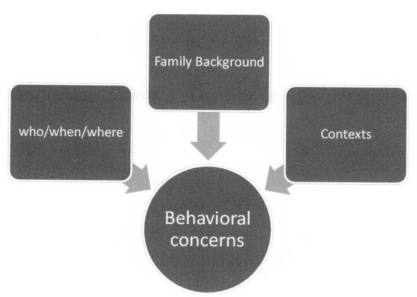

Figure 11.2. Step1: Investigation and Evidence-Gathering Process

Information is a gathered from records, office referrals, parents, teachers, and, if applicable, student reports.

Step 2: What Has Been Done

A common error made by many school teams is that they have not kept a list of all the previous interventions that have been tried and either discarded or forgotten. The team seeks out specifics about what worked, what didn't, and what might have worked if delivered differently and/or monitored differently or even reinforced differently. This list is a collection of ideas and strategies to help educators not repeat the same mistakes around specific strategies.

Step 3: Ask Questions

This step challenges the team's ability to use its analytical and questioning skills. The team needs to have answers to all of its questions before proceeding to the fourth step. Questions will focus on whether medical diagnosis is present. If so, what is it

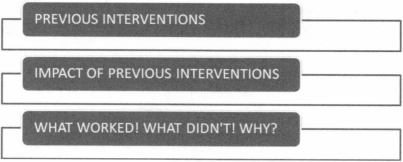

PREVIOUS INTERVENTIONS

IMPACT OF PREVIOUS INTERVENTIONS

WHAT WORKED! WHAT DIDN'T! WHY?

Figure 11.3. Step 2: Evaluation of Interventions

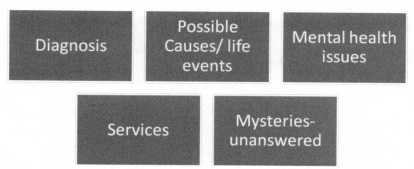

Figure 11.4. *Step 3: Factors Influencing and Impacting Present Behavioral Functioning*

and how is it manifested? What are the side effects and the medication needed?

This second question revolves around the issue of environmental factors: What is truly happening in this child's life that is the catalyst or trigger for the behavioral acting out? Are there mental health issues—depression, anxiety, or conduct disorders? Where is the evidence? Are there any medical or psychological evaluations available? What kinds of services has this individual received in and out of the school environment? Once identified, what were the results, if any? The mysteries unanswered box is a category where all unanswered questions go until an answer is found. Team members are then assigned to find out the answers and bring them back to the team meeting.

Step 4: Respond

In step 4, all the questions and evidence have been answered and substantiated. It is now time to look at what types of interventions will best suit the issues or behavioral concerns. The team brainstorms a list of interventions, chooses the ones they believe will have the most impact, and figures out the

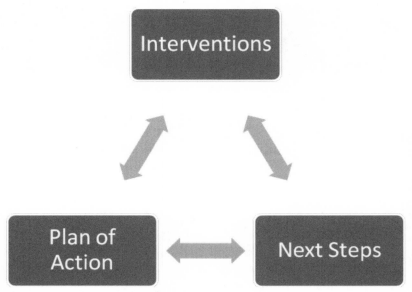

Figure 11.5.   Step 4: Action Planning

plan of action and the next steps. In the plan of action, all the details around the where, how, who, and when are figured out and documented. Team members plan the execution of the action plan and begin thinking about the next steps to creating collaboration with the family and service providers.

Step 5: Evaluate

The plan from step 4 should be monitored and delivered for about two weeks at a minimum and a maximum of one month. Evidence needs to be gathered and analyzed by the team. At this meeting there is ongoing evaluation of what is working and what isn't, and specifics of the plan are revisited and re-programmed into a new plan of action. If the plan is success-ful, monitoring and ongoing encouragement are needed.

In their discussions, the team must think ahead in terms of how they can provide opportunities for a student to have new beginnings. They must meet with the student at some point to discuss what new beginnings are available and how the team will support the student in attaining a fresh start. If the new beginnings require additional skill training, services, parental influence, mentors, coaches, and so on, the goal is to get the student focused on improving the quality of his or her life and relationships. There are many troubled students who can turn their world around. This model is set up in a way that students can be successful, provided they have the right team of adults to guide them. Success only can occur if adults in a student's life are invested in teaching and providing the necessary skills to achieve the goal of being a fully functioning member of society.

In conclusion, this model can become a schoolwide approach to dealing with students with behavior issues. It can be used for individual students as well as groups of students with the same issues. The model can be implemented easily by school teams and with extended practice the time

Figure 11.6.   Step 5: New Beginnings—Evaluation and Futures Planning

factor becomes less of an issue as the team becomes more proficient at finding the correct answers to guide their interventions.

Programs for Schools

The following section will highlight a variety of school curriculum programs that are meant to help schools provide guidance and teaching in the hope of providing dysfunctional students as well as functional students the skills to be better citizens and have more social responsibility and personal management awareness. The author does not endorse one program over another. The selection of a particular program will depend on the specific needs of the school and community. These programs are provided as options only.

Educating for Human Dignity

Where to begin the education on human dignity and the rights of others? Betty Reardon created a K–12 teaching resource titled Educating for Human Dignity: Learning about Rights and Responsibilities. The premise of this curriculum is that it is values-based and conceptual rather than issue- or problem-centered. It assumes that the social problems at all levels, local through global, are as much a matter of ethics as they are of structures, as personal and social as they are political and economic. She believes that more extensive and detailed human rights curricula are needed to address the issues that many youths have today.

The resource offers a curriculum framework and rationale, resource listings, and sample lesson materials to facilitate human rights education in elementary and secondary schools as well as teacher education institutions. It is intended to be suggestive rather than definitive. The lesson plans are presented by grade level, not topic or subject level.

The curriculum is based on interrelated values: Human dignity and integrity as the center of the wheel while economic equity, equality of opportunity, democratic participation, freedom of person, sustaining/able environment all flow into the center as part of the emotional and behavioral involvement and learning.

Reardon developed a developmental sequence for core concepts and content. Below, you will find the developmental level, core concept and values, issues and problems that are presented. She maintains that if the skills are taught at the right level, children and youth will be less likely to act out in aggression or violence and be better citizens.

Developmental Level: Early Childhood (Ages Five to Eight), Grades Kindergarten to Three

Core concept/values: Rules, order, respect, fairness, diversity, cooperation, personal responsibility.

Issues or problem: Inequality, unfairness, harm.

Developmental Level: Later Childhood (Ages Nine to Eleven), Grades Four to Six

Core concept/values: Law, citizenship, community rights, charter, constitution, freedom, declaration, social responsibility.

Issues or problem: Prejudice, discrimination, poverty, injustice.

Developmental Level: Adolescence, (Ages Twelve to Fourteen), Grades Six to Nine

Core concept/values: Justice, equality, equity, conventions, covenants, global responsibility, international law.

Issues or problem: Ethnocentrism, racism, sexism, authoritarianism, colonialism, hunger.

Developmental Level: Youth (Ages Fourteen to Seventeen), Grades Nine to Twelve

Core concept/values: Moral exclusion, moral responsibility, moral inclusion, global citizenship, ecological responsibility.

Issues or problem: Ethnocide, genocide, torture, political repression, environmental abuse.

As values curricula serve to identify and illuminate human problems and human rights, standards serve to diagnose and overcome social wrongs so that particular wrongs can be used as vehicles for learning that will lead students to explore and develop human values and to confront and resolve social problems. The curriculum is vested in helping children and youth develop respect for people, all people no matter what, when, or who. The program develops social responsibility and the idea that cooperative relationships are the most advantageous to all members of a community or society.

Peace Games Curriculum

Peace Games empowers children to create their own safe classrooms and communities by forming partnerships with elementary schools, families, young adult volunteers, and community partners. The goals of the program are to (a) empower children with skills, knowledge, relationships, and opportunities to be peacemakers; (b) engage all community members to support children as peacemakers; (c) inspire a new generation of educators and activists; and (d) change how society thinks about violence and young people.

Peace Games is a model for lasting school climate change that engages a whole school community to support children as peacemakers. Using games and student-driven community service projects, students build skills for peacemaking (cooperation, communication, and conflict resolution), and work to make their school better. The goal is to empower children so that they may create their own safe school community. Peace Games is unique because the program begins when kids are only four years old. The experiential curriculum is designed to match state academic frameworks, is taught by young adult volunteers, and is reinforced by teachers in students' daily routines. The program goes beyond violence prevention to promote peace and justice. Peace Games is located in Boston, and additional information is available at www.peacegames.org.

Social-Emotional Learning Curricula

These curricula were developed to deal with the issues of bullying in the schools. The harmful effects of bullying as well as other forms of social isolation on school climate and student achievement have had devastating implications for many students, including students who have become shooters. Many schools have explored and implemented schoolwide programs to promote social and emotional learning, prevent bullying, and nurture positive peer relationships.

The following guidelines are recommended by Donna San Antonio (director of the Appalachian Mountain Teen Project) and Elizabeth Salzfass (program and evaluation coordinator for Responsive Advocacy for Life and Learning in Youth).

Look for a curriculum that:

1. Becomes part of a schoolwide and communitywide discussion with parents on values and beliefs about how to treat one another and policies that reflect these values.
2. Possesses developmentally and culturally appropriate social dilemmas for discussion.
3. Challenges the idea that aggression and bullying are inevitable and expected behavior. Demonstrates how people can resolve tensions and disagreements without losing face by giving detailed examples of people who responded to violence in an actively nonviolent manner.

4. Encourages students to express their feelings and experiences concerning bullying and enables students to generate realistic and credible ways to stay safe.
5. Supports critical analysis of the issues and rejects explanations of behavior based on stereotypes.
6. Helps children and teens become critical consumers of popular culture.
7. Addresses all types of bullying.
8. Discusses how bullying reflects broader societal injustice.
9. Gives ideas for what adults in the school can do as part of a whole-school effort.

Here is a list of several online social-emotional learning curricula:

1. The Collaborative for Academic, Social and Emotional Learning (CASEL). The mission of the program is to advance the science of social and emotional learning and to expand coordinated, evidence-based social-emotional learning. Resources include the Sustainable School-wide Social and Emotional Learning implementation guide and toolkit. See www.casel.org.
2. The Safetyzone is a clearinghouse for information and material related to school safety. There are eight guides to download at www.safetyzone.org/index.html.
3. The Olweus Bullying Prevention Program is a program for preventing or reducing bullying in elementary and middle schools. It trains students, teachers, staff, and parents to take a stand on bullying. See www.clemson.edu/olweus.
4. Committee for Children provides classroom programs that focus on the topics of youth violence, bullying, child abuse, personal safety, and emergent literacy. Includes information on Steps to Respect, a bullying

prevention program for grades three to six. See www.cfchildren.org.

Life Space Crisis Intervention (LSCI) Program

The LSCI program is a process that helps children and youths learn how to deal with a crisis. This program looks at crises in mental health, schools, and the courts. It provides very specific interventions on how to deal with a variety of issues and situations through understanding of conflict, triggers, and other factors. The program includes a variety of specific activities and procedures to deal with students in a crisis situation. It offers a series of best practices depending on the crisis.

The program helps to deal with the dysfunction of the family and the shocking social problems in communities. It can provide information on problems such as alcoholism, drug use, suicide, gang warfare, rape, physical and psychological abuse, crime, parental neglect and abandonment, brutality as an entertainment, and poverty. Violence is a common experience for many students today. This program helps educators teach skills to students to better deal with the list of issues presented above.

Peace Builders Program

This curriculum is for kindergarten to fifth-grade students. The aim of the program is to change school climate. Goals are to promote prosocial behavior, reduce child aggression, and improve social competence. Five universal principles are taught: (a) praise people; (b) avoid put-downs; (c) seek wise people as advisers and friends; (d) notice and correct hurts we cause; and (e) adults are to reinforce and model behaviors. Outcomes of this program are increased social competence, fewer aggressive behaviors, and fewer fight-related injuries to the nurse's office. See www.peace builders.com.

Second Step Program

This curriculum is usually for second and third grades. It is a curriculum-based program (thirty lessons) consisting of activities to teach empathy, impulse control, problem solving, and anger management. See www.cfchildren.org.

Richmond Youth against Violence: Responding in Peaceful and Positive Ways Program

This curriculum is for sixth grade. It is a lecture-based curriculum focusing on imparting knowledge about ways in which the host, agent, and environment contribute to youth violence. Sessions focus on building trust, respect for individual differences, nature of violence and risk factors, anger management, personal values, precipitants and consequences of fighting, and nonviolent alternatives to fighting. See www.prevent youthviolence.vcu/index.html.

Students for Peace Project

This curriculum is for middle school students (sixth to eighth grades). The curriculum is based on developing and implementing peace-related activities. It uses the Second Step Program for writing prompts. It focuses on developing peer mediation and training students to mediate conflicts, formally and informally, among peers. It trains peers helping peers by having students meet one-on-one with those who request help with personal problems. It also involves parents through the use of newsletters.

The Seattle Social Development Project

This program is for first to twelfth grade, combining parent and teacher training. The teachers receive instruction that emphasizes classroom management, interactive teaching, and cooperative learning. Curriculum involves skills around communication, decision-making, negotiation, and conflict resolution. Parents receive training in areas of family management, communication between home and school, how to create positive home environments, and how to support their children's academic progress. Sessions are given to help parents create family positions on drugs and encourage children's resistance skills. See http://dpts.washington.edu/sdrg.

Child Development Project

This curriculum is for third- to sixth-grade students. It is a comprehensive model focused on creating cooperative and supportive school environments. Classroom components include: (a) staff training in cooperative learning, (b) implementation of a model that fosters cross-grade buddy activities, (c) a developmental approach to discipline that fosters self-control, and (d) a model to engage students in classroom norm-setting and decision-making. Schoolwide community building activities are used to promote school bonding and parent involvement activities such as interactive homework assignments that reinforce the family-school partnership. See www.devstu .org/cdp/index.html.

Bullying Prevention Program

This curriculum is for fourth- to seventh-grade students. Core components of the program are the school, class, and individual levels. At the school level the following actions are taken: (a) distribution of anonymous student questionnaires assessing the nature and prevalence of bullying, (b) training staff on program, (c) adoption of positive and negative consequences for student behavior, and (d) holding staff discussion groups and involving parents. At the class level, the following actions are recommended: (a) reinforcement of schoolwide rules; (b) holding classroom meetings; (c) students increase levels of knowledge and empathy; and (d) informational meetings with parents. At the individual level, the following are put into practice: (a) interventions with children who bully; (b) intervention with children who are bullied; and (c) discussions with parents. See www.clemson.edu/olweus.

Brain Power Program

This curriculum is for third- to sixth-grade students, focusing on attribution retraining. The training is designed to strengthen aggressive boys' ability to accurately detect the intentions of others and increase the likelihood that aggressive boys will first attribute negative outcomes to accidental causes and work at understanding these ideas. The program helps boys link appropriate nonaggressive behavioral responses to ambiguously caused negative social outcomes. Contact hudley@education.uscb.edu for information.

FAST Track Families and Schools Together

This curriculum is for first- to fifth-grade students. The program used is PATHS (Promoting Alternative Thinking Strategies). It is administered to classrooms in fifty-seven lessons, one half-hour a week, two to three times a week. The program builds skills for understanding and communicating emotions, skills to increase positive social behavior, and skills to increase self-control and social problem-solving skills. The program is presented through direct instruction, discussion, modeling stories, and video. This program also works with at-risk kindergarteners identified as having emotional and behavioral issues. See www.fasttrackproject.org.

Successful schoolwide intervention programs have the following core implementation characteristics:

1. They raise the awareness and responsibility of students, teachers, and parents regarding the types of violence in the school.
2. They create clear guidelines and rules for the entire school.
3. They target the various social systems in the school and clearly communicate to the entire school community procedures to be followed before, during, and after violent events.
4. They focus on getting school staff, students, and parents involved in the program.
5. The interventions fit easily into the normal flow and mission of the school.
6. They use faculty, staff, and parents in the school setting to plan, implement, and sustain the program.
7. They increase monitoring and supervision in nonclassroom areas. (Astor et al., 2005)

It is important that a school chooses the right program for its needs. Each school, as we know, is unique and has a different set of problems that require a different set of approaches. A program must be chosen on very specific criteria: What are the problems that the program will address? What are the mechanisms for data collection on effectiveness? What methods will be used for monitoring of the delivery and implementation of the program?

In conclusion, a program that is adapted to the needs of an individual school and involves the entire community is most likely to be successful. A clear match needs to occur between the goals of the programs and the needs of the particular school and community. It is in creating a partnership that school shootings will become an event of the past. By arming students with skills, training, awareness, and knowledge we can disarm them in the long run.

12

School Shootings and the Media

We live in a society where we depend on technology to keep us informed. Ever since the telephone, radio, and television were invented, we have relied on these sources to educate the masses. The printed word in the form of newspapers became a major source of information once the masses were literate and could understand the text. These forms of media have been a staple of our lives.

Life in the media is fast-paced, short-lived, and often speeds by at the speed of light. An event is news one day, maybe a second day, and replaced by something more sensational or horrific on the third day. When a school shooting occurs, it becomes the focus of all television news networks. They replay the incident over and over. They provide the viewer or the reader with graphic pictures that personalize the tragedy for the audience. We see the images repeated consistently. The American public becomes fascinated with these images of gore. What is it about the event that speaks to our morbid interests?

Why are Americans so enthralled by graphic images? It is believed by many that Americans have become immune to violence because it is part of life here. People see shootings and murders on the six o'clock news daily. They walk in communities where people are shot, wounded, or killed. People have come to expect that violence inhabits their community and that there are many unsafe places in this country. It is a by-product of poverty and drugs.

Psychologically speaking, people are curious and want to see. The prime example is observing the behaviors of people when there has been a car accident; people slow down to see someone dead or injured or what the police are doing. People want front-row seats to see exactly what has happened, and in their opinion, the media is providing a service. They are only giving the audience what they want. They are not at fault for providing news; they are not responsible for how people interpret their reporting. They are providing the facts as they see them. They believe that reporting the incidents leads to better information awareness.

One needs only to step back and look at the news reporting of a school shooting to see the lack of professionalism or insufficient evidence provided to know that children and youth who are watching will be more confused. Children who have been in a school where the shooting has occurred are at risk emotionally and psychologically of developing post-traumatic stress disorder because of what they are seeing on their televisions.

Television networks need to provide guidance to their audience and put out disclaimers. They need to warn the public that some of the images may be disturbing to children and that if families are going to watch, an adult should be present to explain the happenings and address questions and fears children may have.

In this country, freedom of speech trumps many other rights. What about the rights of the victim's family? Do they not deserve to be respected? What about the rights of the shooter's family? Can they not be protected as well? It seems that the shooter becomes the focal point of all the interpretation of why the event occurred.

Journalists and reporters throw forth theories without having solid evidence of the causes for the school shooting in the first place. There are many occasions when false or inaccurate information has been put to press or live on television because there is a belief that the public must know what is happening now.

In hundreds of reports of school shootings, on several occasions the media inaccurately reported the facts and responses to the school shooting. Well-intentioned media created sensational stories that sold newspapers and made for great television. But where is the ethical responsibility on the part of these reporters? Is the goal to make a quick buck or get great ratings? The answer unfortunately is yes. The moguls who run their media empires are very rich because they have learned to capitalize on the tragedy of human behavior and actions. A good story sells.

To be fair, there are journalists out there who are credible, honest, and report the information that leads to public education and helps advance the education of a nation on several topics and subject matters. These individuals ask very poignant and directed questions after a tragedy and are often instrumental in getting agencies or organizations to reexamine their policies and procedures.

Good changes can come out of their investigative journalism. How do we ensure that professionalism overrides sensationalism? We make the networks and newspapers responsible for what they televise and publish. We have very strict codes of behavior. We set a standard and stick to it. We make the media accountable.

History of School Shootings

In this next section you will find a short summary of school shootings. All of these shootings have been documented in newspapers and on television. I will begin with the earliest documented cases and finish with the most recent events. I challenge you to seek out how the media reported the story and what became of the reports. You will find some interesting insights. Many of these lists were retrieved from the Internet, on sites such as the World News Report Agency and the indyStar.com website.

1970s

Jan. 29, 1979: Brenda Spencer, sixteen, opened fire with a .22-caliber rifle at an elementary school across the street from her San Diego home. She killed two people and wounded seven because she "didn't like Mondays." She is in prison.

At this point in time school shootings were rare and almost unheard of in the American school system. Schools were still wide open to anyone and everyone in the community. People had a sense of freedom and security. Schools were welcoming places where all were protected and nurtured to learn.

1980s

The following excerpts were retrieved from www.indystar .com.

Jan. 21, 1985: James Alan Kearbey, fourteen, armed with an M1-A semiautomatic rifle and a .357-caliber handgun, killed the principal and wounded two teachers and a student at his Goddard (Kansas) junior high school. He pleaded no contest and served seven years in a state youth facility.

May 20, 1988: Laurie Dann, thirty, shot six students at a Winnetka, Illinois, elementary school, killing one second-grader. She then shot a man in a nearby house before committing suicide.

Sept. 26, 1988: James Wilson, nineteen, opened fire in a Greenwood, South Carolina, elementary school. He shot seven students and two teachers. Two eight-year-old girls died.

Jan. 17, 1989: Patrick Purdy, twenty-six, armed with an AK-47 assault rifle, opened fire on a playground at a Stockton, California, elementary school. Five children died and twenty-nine children and one teacher were wounded before Purdy killed himself.

At the end of the 1980s we had been informed of the shootings listed above. The school system became increasingly aware that a shooting could occur in its community school. Educators became more proactive at speaking about this emerging issue. Schools began formulating crisis plans. At this point in history the problem had not reached epidemic levels. People were concerned, but not frightened.

Little did they know that the next decade would bring a flurry of school shootings and with it a change of culture and attitude around school and societal violence! The nightmare was about to get worse. The horrors that were brooding in the minds of the adolescents were only in the planning stages and had yet to be realized. The decade of violence began and in so doing influenced American education in a dramatic way. Crisis led to forced and immediate change.

1990s

The following excerpts were retrieved from www.indystar .com.

May 1, 1992: Eric Houston, twenty, killed four people and wounded ten in a siege at his former high school in Olivehurst, California. The attack was said to be in retaliation for a failing grade. Houston was convicted and sentenced to death.

Jan. 18, 1993: Scott Pennington, seventeen, walked into Deanna McDavid's English class at East Carter High School in Grayson, Kentucky, and shot her in the head. He then shot janitor Marvin Hicks. Pennington was sentenced.

Feb. 2, 1996: Fourteen-year-old Barry Loukaitis walked into algebra class with a hunting rifle in his trench coat and opened fire, killing the teacher and two students. A third student was injured during the shooting at a junior high school in Moses Lake, Washington.

Feb. 19, 1997: Sixteen-year-old Evan Ramsey opened fire with a shotgun in a common area at a Bethel, Alaska, high school, killing the principal and a student and wounding two others. Ramsey was sentenced to two ninety-nine-year prison terms.

Oct. 1, 1997: Sixteen-year-old outcast Luke Woodham of Pearl, Mississippi, was sentenced to life in prison for killing his mother, and then going to Pearl High School and shooting nine students. Two students died, including the suspect's ex-girlfriend.

Dec. 1, 1997: Three students were killed and five others wounded as they took part in a prayer circle in a hallway at Heath High School in West Paducah, Kentucky. Michael Carneal, fourteen, described as emotionally immature, plead guilty but mentally ill, and was sentenced to life. One of the wounded girls was paralyzed.

Mar. 24, 1998: Four girls and a teacher were shot to death and ten others wounded during a false fire alarm at Westside Middle School in Jonesboro, Arkansas. Two boys, Andrew Golden, eleven, and Mitchell Johnson, thirteen, were accused of setting off the alarm and then opening fire from nearby woods.

Apr. 24, 1998: A forty-eight-year-old science teacher was shot to death in front of students at a graduation dance in Edinboro, Pennsylvania. Andrew Wurst, a fourteen-year-old student at James W. Parker Middle School, was charged. The killer was later described as depressed, alienated, and a boy who never smiled.

Apr. 28, 1998: Two teenage boys were shot to death and a third was wounded as they played basketball at a Pomona, California, elementary school hours after classes had ended. An unidentified fourteen-year-old boy was charged.

May 19, 1998: Three days before graduation, eighteen-year-old honor student Jacob Davis allegedly opened fire in a parking lot at Lincoln County High School in Fayetteville, Tennessee, killing a classmate who was dating his ex-girl-friend.

May 21, 1998: A fifteen-year-old girl was shot and wounded at a suburban Houston high school when a gun in the backpack of a seventeen-year-old boy discharged.

May 21, 1998: Miles Fox, fifteen, died from a self-inflicted gunshot wound to the head in Onalaska, Washington. He boarded a high school bus with a gun in hand, ordered his girlfriend off the bus, and took her to his home where he shot himself.

May 21, 1998: Two students were killed and more than twenty other people wounded when Kip Kinkel, fifteen, opened fire at Thurston High School's cafeteria in Springfield, Oregon. Earlier that day, he killed his parents. He had been expelled the day before for bringing a gun to school.

June 15, 1998: A male teacher and a female guidance counselor were shot in a hallway at a Richmond, Virginia, high school. Neither was seriously injured.

Apr. 20, 1999: Columbine High School students Dylan Klebold, seventeen, and Eric Harris, eighteen, went on a shooting rampage, killing twelve of their classmates and one teacher, a Hoosier native, in Littleton, Colorado. Klebold and Harris then killed themselves. The massacre was the bloodiest school shooting in U.S. history.

May 20, 1999: T. J. Solomon, fifteen, opened fire at Heritage High School in Conyers, Georgia, wounding six students. Solomon pleaded guilty but mentally ill and was sentenced to forty years in prison.

Nov. 19, 1999: A thirteen-year-old girl was shot in the head in school at Deming, New Mexico. She died the next day. Twelve-year-old Victor Cordova Jr. pleaded guilty to the shooting.

Dec. 6, 1999: Seth Trickey, thirteen, fired at least fifteen rounds at Fort Gibson Middle School in Fort Gibson, Oklahoma, wounding four classmates. He was convicted on seven assault charges.

The 1990s was a decade that had many school shootings. Looking at the list of events one would believe that it had become an epidemic. Some educators would agree that students were using violence as a coping mechanism. Schools became increasingly frightened. Communities revolted with policies and demands to make schools safer. Uniformed police and security personnel became part of the structure and environment of schools, especially high schools.

Some schools became prison-like in terms of security. At the dawn of the new millennium, educators seemed to be relaxing around the issue of school safety. Little did they know that the new age would bring even more shootings! The time of peace was no longer. Schools have become war zones in many communities.

The New Millennium: 2000–2008

The following excerpts were retrieved from www.indystar.com, except as noted.

Feb. 29, 2000: A first-grade boy at Buell Elementary School in Mount Morris Township, Michigan, fatally shot classmate Kayla Rolland, six, after the two children had a verbal spat. He took a .32-caliber handgun from his uncle's home, where he was living.

Mar. 10, 2000: Nineteen-year-old Stacy Smalls and sixteen-year-old Ramone Kimble died from gunshot wounds they suffered as they were leaving a dance honoring the Savannah, Georgia, Beach High School girls' basketball state championship team. Darrell Ingram, nineteen, was arrested and charged with murder and aggravated assault.

May 26, 2000: In Lake Worth, Florida, thirteen-year-old honor student Nathaniel Brazill shot a teacher in the face, killing him. Police said the seventh-grader had been sent home for throwing water balloons and returned to the school with a handgun he found in his grandfather's dresser.

Sept. 26, 2000: A thirteen-year-old and a fifteen-year-old were critically wounded when they shot each other with the same gun. The shootings occurred during a fight at Woodson Middle School in New Orleans. The gun had been slipped through a fence to one of the students by a thirteen-year-old who had been expelled from the school.

Oct. 24, 2000: An armed teenager briefly held a classroom full of children and a teacher hostage at Pioneer Elementary School in Glendale, Arizona, before surrendering to authorities. There were no injuries.

Jan. 17, 2001: Juan Matthews, seventeen, died after being shot three times while standing in front of Lake Clifton Eastern High School in Baltimore.

Feb. 2, 2001: Two students and teachers were reportedly grazed by gunfire at Osborn High School in Detroit. The victims were not seriously hurt, and no suspect was caught.

Mar. 5, 2001: Fifteen-year-old Charles Andrew Williams was arrested for killing two classmates, and wounding thirteen other people, at Santana High School in Santee, California. In August 2002, he received a fifty-year-to-life sentence.

Mar. 7, 2001: An eighth-grade girl shot a thirteen-year-old classmate during lunch at Bishop Neumann Junior-Senior High School in Williamsport, Pennsylvania. The suspect was arrested and the injuries were not considered life-threatening.

Mar. 22, 2001: Four students and two teachers were wounded at Granite Hills High School in El Cajon, California. None of the injuries were life-threatening. One of the wounded students, eighteen-year-old Jason Hoffman, was the alleged assailant. The shooting took place in a San Diego suburb just seven miles from the March 5th high school shooting.

Mar. 30, 2001: Neal Boyd IV, sixteen, was shot to death outside Lew Wallace High School in Gary, Indiana, where he was a student. Seventeen-year-old Donald R. Burt Jr. was arrested, convicted, and sentenced to fifty-seven years in prison.

Nov. 13, 2001: Chris Buschbacher, seventeen, went to the Caro (Michigan) Learning Center armed with a .22-caliber rifle and a 20-gauge shotgun, and took a student and a teacher hostage. During a three-hour standoff, he fired two shots. The hostages were eventually released, but Buschbacher, who was reportedly despondent over a breakup with his girlfriend, shot himself as police prepared to enter the building.

Jan. 15, 2002: Two students at Martin Luther King Jr. High School in Manhattan were seriously wounded when a teenager opened fire at the school.

Apr. 14, 2003: Gunmen armed with an AK-47 rifle and a handgun opened fire in the packed gymnasium of John Mc-Donogh Senior High School in New Orleans. Jonathan Williams, fifteen, was killed and three girls were wounded in a spray of bullets. It was thought to be a revenge killing for an earlier murder. A loaded handgun was found on the victim. Four suspects were arrested.

Apr. 24, 2003: In Red Lion, Pennsylvania, fourteen-year-old James Sheets shot and killed his middle school principal, Eugene Segro, in a crowded school cafeteria and then killed himself.

Sept. 24, 2003: Aaron Rollins, seventeen, was killed and Seth Bartell, fourteen, was critically wounded when fifteen-year-old John Jason McLaughlin walked out of a locker room at Rocori High School in Cold Spring, Minnesota, and shot them with a .22-caliber gun he had in his gym bag. Bartell died Oct. 10.

Sept. 26, 2003: A thirteen-year-old boy fired a 9-mm semi-automatic handgun into the ceiling of a Cleveland County, North Carolina, middle school. He also fired one shot into the closed door of a classroom filled with students. No one was injured.

Oct. 30, 2003: Sixteen-year-old Devin Fowlkes was shot to death in front of Anacostia Senior High School in Washington, D.C., as he left a homecoming dance along with a crowd of students. Another student was slightly injured. A fifteen-year-old, who said he was aiming at someone else, was arrested and charged with murder.

Nov. 14, 2003: A fifteen-year-old student accidently fired a handgun outside East Mecklenburg High School, North Carolina, cafeteria, injuring two students.

Jan. 13, 2004: Following an argument, a nineteen-year-old entered Northern High School in Detroit and shot Aaron Wilson, eighteen, six times in the leg. Neither teen was a student at the school.

Feb. 2, 2004: Seventeen-year-old James Richardson was shot to death in Ballou Senior High School in Washington, D.C., during second period. The shooting resulted from a confrontation with another student who was arrested.

Feb. 11, 2004: Ten-year-old Faheem Thomas-Childs was shot in the face outside T. M. Peirce Elementary School in Philadelphia. He died six days after the shooting. He was caught in a shootout between two rival gangs. The gun battle unleashed nearly one hundred shots in the area as children were arriving at school. A school crossing guard also was injured. Two men were arrested for the shooting.

Apr. 3, 2004: A shot was fired from a passing car through the glass front door of the Accelerated Learning and Transition Academy in Houston. About two hundred students were in the school at the time, but no one was injured.

May 7, 2004: Four teenagers leaving a charity basketball game at their Randallstown, Maryland, high school were wounded, one critically, in a drive-by shooting. Among the suspects was a seventeen-year-old student at the school who had been involved in an earlier incident over a girl.

Nov. 24, 2004: James Lewerke, a fifteen-year-old student at Valparaiso High School in northern Indiana, pulled two large knives out of his pants and stabbed seven of his classmates. None of the injuries were life-threatening.

Mar. 21, 2005: Jeff Weise, sixteen, shot to death his grandfather and his grandfather's girlfriend and then went to his high school in Red Lake, Minnesota, where he killed a security guard, a teacher, and five students, and wounded seven others before killing himself.

Nov. 8, 2005: Assistant principal Ken Bruce was killed and two other administrators seriously wounded when Kenny Bartley, a fifteen-year-old student, opened fire in a Jacksboro, Tennessee, high school.

Aug. 14, 2006: A twenty-five-year-old security guard from Moreno Valley, California, was found shot to death around 6:15 p.m. at an elementary school he had been hired to guard from vandals and taggers. No students were at the school as the incident occurred during summer break.

Aug. 17, 2006: A twenty-one-year-old male was shot and killed in an Austin, Texas, middle school parking lot in what police believed to be a gang-related dispute. The incident occurred during evening hours as a group of youth were preparing for a *quinceañera*, a fifteenth-birthday-party celebration. A twenty-year-old and a seventeen-year-old were subsequently arrested.

Aug. 24, 2006: In Essex, Vermont, a twenty-seven-year-old male shot and killed a fifty-six-year-old second-grade teacher in her elementary school classroom. The man was looking for his ex-girlfriend, who also was a teacher at the school and had reportedly broken up with him the night before the incident. A fifty-two-year-old female first-grade teacher also was shot through a window. The suspect had reportedly shot and killed his ex-girlfriend's mother, age fifty-seven. The staff members in the building reportedly moved to lock down the school.

Sept. 13, 2006: A sixteen-year-old male high school student in Van Nuys, California, was shot and killed across the street from his high school around 3:40 p.m., a half hour after classes let out, in what police believed was a gang-related shooting.

Sept. 27, 2006: Duane Morrison, fifty-three, took six girls hostage at Platte Canyon High School in Bailey, Colorado, molesting them and holding them for hours before fatally shooting one girl and then himself. After releasing some hostages, the male shot at S.W.A.T. officers as they entered the classroom, and then shot a sixteen-year-old female hostage who later died from her wounds. The suspect shot himself with one round to commit suicide as S.W.A.T. officers who were entering the room also shot him three times.

Sept. 29, 2006: Eric Hainstock, fifteen, took two guns into his Cazenovia, Wisconsin, pre-kindergarten to twelfth-grade school and fatally shot the principal before being captured and arrested. He shot the principal after walking into the school with a shotgun and a handgun taken from his family's gun cabinet, according to reports. He reportedly was confronted by the school's custodian, teachers, and students, who tried to wrestle the gun away from him. The custodian said the male was a special education student who said he was there to kill someone.

When confronted by the school's forty-nine-year-old principal, the teen shot the principal in the head, chest, and leg. After being shot, the principal wrestled the male to the ground and swept the gun away. The principal died at the hospital several hours later. The teen reportedly had been harassed by other students and believed that teachers and the principal were not doing anything about it. The teen was said to have told another student that the principal "would not make it through homecoming." The teen was in police custody and will be charged as an adult.

Oct. 2, 2006: Charles Carl Roberts, thirty-two, took ten girls hostage in an Amish school in Nickel Mines, Pennsylvania, killing five of them before killing himself.

Oct. 17, 2006: In Katy, Texas, a sixteen-year-old male high school sophomore committed suicide by shooting himself with a handgun in the school's cafeteria courtyard.

Oct. 19, 2006: In Orlando, Florida, a fifteen-year-old male high school student was stabbed with a large serrated knife by a seventeen-year-old male student at the school, according to reports. The incident happened on the east side of the school near the sidewalk in the area of the school buses, reports said. The two males fought and the victim was stabbed during the fight, after which he was transported to the hospital where he subsequently died. Students reported the two males may have had a conflict over a girl.

Oct. 31, 2006: A thirty-nine-year-old male school security officer in Knoxville, Tennessee, was shot and killed around 10:20 p.m. in his high school's parking lot while assigned to patrol the school to prevent Halloween vandalism. A thirty-nine-year-old suspect was arrested after a police pursuit of the suspect who stole the victim's car. The suspect claimed he was a homeless man from Virginia, but police reported he was from Tennessee and may have had pending charges for another murder. School officials reported that the officer was a very close member of the school "family" and connected well with students at the high school, who were torn by his loss. Grief counselors were to be on hand the next day at the school.

Nov. 29, 2006: A sixteen-year-old male high school student from Houston was shot to death behind the school while walking to school in the morning. Reports indicated the incident was believed to be gang-related.

Dec. 12, 2006: A sixteen-year-old male high school student in Springfield Township, Pennsylvania, shot and killed himself with an AK-47 in the hallway of his high school. The student, reportedly despondent over his grades, had the gun concealed in a camouflage duffle bag and fired one round in the ceiling to warn other students to get out of the way before he committed suicide.

Jan. 3, 2007: An eighteen-year-old male high school student in Tacoma, Washington, was arrested for shooting and killing a seventeen-year-old male student at their school. The suspect allegedly shot the victim in the face and then stood over him, firing twice more.

Jan. 19, 2007: A fifteen-year-old male high school student in Sudbury, Massachusetts, was stabbed to death by a sixteen-year-old male student in the hallway of their high school. The two reportedly got into a fight in a restroom which spilled out in the hallway, at which time the suspect stabbed the victim twice with a long knife, once in the abdomen and once in the heart.

Jan. 26, 2007: An eighteen-year-old male from Los Angeles was shot in the upper body three times and died while playing basketball in a middle school gym around 5:50 p.m. Police were seeking three suspects who fled after the shooting. The identity of the victim and his association with the school was not immediately made clear. Dozens of people were present but not injured, according to reports.

Feb. 8, 2007: An eighteen-year-old male high school student from Prineville, Oregon, committed suicide with a gunshot wound to the head in the high school's parking lot. He was found by a student around 2:30 p.m.

Feb. 17, 2007: A twenty-six-year-old male from Flint, Michigan, was shot in the head in a parking lot of an elementary school where he was visiting for an adult basketball league that rented the gym. The male later died. Police arrested three people.

Feb. 26, 2007: A fifteen-year-old male high school student from St. Louis was killed and a sixteen-year-old male student shot outside the home of an eighteen-year-old student in the afternoon, following an altercation that began earlier in the day at their high school. A crowd gathered outside the home to watch a fight and the eighteen-year-old stood in the door with a baseball bat, according to reports. After rocks and rolled newspapers were thrown at the house, the eighteen-year-old reappeared with a rifle and his fifty-one-year-old mother with a handgun. Both opened fire. The fifteen-year-old was killed and the sixteen-year-old injured. Counselors and additional security measures were put in place at the school for the following days.

Mar. 7, 2007: A sixteen-year-old male high school student from Greenville, Texas, fatally shot himself while in the band hallway area of the school around 7:15 a.m. No other students were injured. More than one hundred parents rushed to the school to remove their children.

Mar. 7, 2007: In Midland, Michigan, a seventeen-year-old male nonstudent shot a seventeen-year-old female student four times and then turned the gun on himself, committing suicide in her high school's parking lot. The female was reportedly an ex-girlfriend of the male. Reports indicated the male drove to the school to talk with the female but was turned away by school officials, after which he called her out to the parking lot to talk with him. He pulled a gun and shot her four times, which was witnessed by the girl's mother who was in her car and drove between them. The female was taken to the hospital and reported to be in serious but stable condition.

Mar. 23, 2007: A seventeen-year-old male high school student from Los Angeles was stabbed to death during a fight outside the school's gym with three other males around 3:00 p.m. The suspects reportedly were sixteen to seventeen years old.

Apr. 16, 2007: Virginia Tech University in Blacksburg, Virginia, was the scene of shooting where thirty-three students and staff were massacred, with another fifteen injured in the academic and residential halls. The shooter was Seung-Hui Cho, who suffered mental health issues. His shootings appear to be random (*New York Times*, April 17, 2007).

Apr. 18, 2007: A sixteen-year-old male high school student from Huntersville, North Carolina, threatened two high school students with a gun in their school's parking lot and then turned the gun on himself, committing suicide. Police alerted four schools in the area, which went into lockdown. Counselors were made available at the school upon the students' return.

May 2, 2007: A thirty-one-year-old female bus driver from Newark, Delaware, was found stabbed to death on her school bus, which was pulled over to the side of the road shortly after she left the school bus depot to start picking up middle school students. A boyfriend reportedly was in custody being interviewed.

May 5, 2007: A fifteen-year-old female high school student from El Maton, Texas, committed suicide by a .38-caliber gunshot to the head in a school restroom. Her body was found by another student from her band class who checked the restroom after the student left and did not return.

June 8, 2007: A sixteen-year-old male student from a military-style charter school academy in Sacramento was shot while he and his eighteen-year-old brother were driving to school. The male was subsequently taken off life support and died. The victim was set to graduate the day of the incident and to receive an honors award, according to reports. A twenty-two-year-old male was arrested in connection with the shooting, which police believe was gang-related.

Sept. 22, 2007: Two university freshmen in from Dover, Delaware, were shot and wounded, one seriously, when an argument that had begun at a university cafeteria resumed on the street.

Nov. 1, 2007: A thirteen-year-old male middle school student from Fresno died as a result of an afterschool fight in a parking lot near the school. The incident reportedly stemmed from an ongoing conflict with a fourteen-year-old male student who was fighting with him. The victim was knocked to the ground and then hit afterwards, and the assailant left. The thirteen-year-old later died from the injuries.

Feb. 15, 2008: At Northern Illinois University in Chicago, Steve Kazmierczak opened fire from the front of a large lecture hall with 120–160 students present. He killed five students and himself, injuring eighteen others. He was armed with a shotgun and three handguns. He recently had stopped taking his medication for his anxiety and other mental health concerns (*New York Times*, February 17, 2008).

We have not completed the millennium and we already have an astounding list of shootings. Is this a predictor of what is to come? Are we faced with impending gloom and doom when it comes to violence in the schools? Schools are now better prepared. Most schools have extensive lockdown procedures and protocols. They have crisis response teams, have built partnerships with local law enforcement, and are ready to jump into action if needed. The goal is to be ready, hoping that the emergency response team never needs to be activated.

School shootings are an excellent gauge of the mental well-being of the society. If children and youth have necessary supports and services to deal with anger, frustration, bullying, and mental health they are less likely to manifest their pain, hopelessness, or anger in the form of violence with a gun. Teaching children and youth to communicate is the key. Helping society to become more nurturing of its young will go a long way toward decreasing the rate of school shootings.

International Shootings

School shootings are not unique to the United States; they do happen elsewhere in the world. The interesting point is that they are very rare and few and far between. Why is that? Is America a more violent place? Are there better gun laws and controls elsewhere? Are children in the rest of the world better able to handle their stress and anger? What is it in this culture that seems to create more shooters?

My theories are that in other countries there is still a large connection between families and their children. There is a bond that exists that supports youth in their time of need and misery. Children are taught from an early age to respect themselves, their teachers, and their communities. There seems to be more teaching around values and morality. Children are taught to seek out their family for problem-solving strategies and to communicate when there are issues. Your family is everything and you must protect them at all cost.

The American family seems to be disenfranchised. Youths worldwide do not seem to have as much access to guns as American youth do. The United States has the highest per capita gun ownership in the world, with Yemen second, and

Finland third. Yet there are very few incidents with guns in those two other countries.

The following are examples of some of the shootings that have occurred in other places worldwide. The source for these is indystar.com.

Mar. 13, 1996: Thomas Hamilton, forty-three, dressed in black and wearing earmuffs to protect himself from the noise, entered an elementary school in Dunblane, Scotland, and sprayed 105 bullets into the gym, striking twenty-nine people before killing himself. Sixteen five- and six-year-olds and a teacher died.

Mar. 30, 1997: Mohammad Ahmad al-Naziri, forty-eight, armed with an assault rifle, opened fire on hundreds of students at two schools in Sanaa, Yemen. Six children and two others died. He was sentenced to death and executed by firing squad one week after the incident.

Apr. 28, 1999: A fourteen-year-old who had been bullied by his classmates, opened fire at W. R. Myers high school in Taber, Alberta, Canada, killing a seventeen-year-old student and wounding another student. The boy, who was obsessed with the Columbine shootings, pleaded guilty to murder and attempted murder, and in November 2000 was sentenced to three years in jail.

Mar. 26, 2001: An arson fire at the Kyanguli Secondary school in Kenya killed sixty-seven students. Two students were charged with murder.

June 8, 2001: Mamoru Takuma forced his way into Ikeda Elementary School in Osaka, Japan, stabbed to death eight students and injured thirteen others. Takuma, who had a long history of mental illness, pleaded guilty to the crimes.

Feb. 19, 2002: A twenty-two-year-old gunman in Munich, Germany, killed his former boss and a foreman at the company that fired him, then went to a high school in a Munich suburb, where he shot the school's headmaster when he was unable to find the teacher he was after. He then shot another teacher in the face and set off homemade bombs, before killing himself.

Apr. 26, 2002: Nineteen-year-old Robert Steinhaeuser, who had been expelled from Johann Gutenberg High School in Erfurt, Germany, returned to the school and shot to death thirteen teachers, two students, and a police officer, before killing himself.

Apr. 29, 2002: Seventeen-year-old Dragoslav Petkovic opened fire with a handgun shortly after noon at his high school in Vlasenica, Bosnia-Herzegovina, killing one teacher and wounding another, before taking his own life.

July 10, 2007: In Kabul, Afghanistan, ten young girls were shot when they left school early. The gunmen randomly shot at everything. They fled on foot in a panic and disappeared in a wheat field (*New York Times*, July 10, 2007).

Nov. 8, 2007: In Tuusula, Finland, an eighteen-year-old student killed seven children and a principal when he opened fire at a school. He posted a video on YouTube foreshadowing the massacre. The shooter was Pekka-Eric Auvienen. He basically moved systemically through the school hallways, knocking on doors and shooting through the doors (*New York Times*, November 8, 2007).

Dec. 12, 2007: Two fourteen-year-old boys in Gurgaon, India, brought a gun to school and confronted a third student in a school hall and took turns shooting him at close range. School shootings are virtually unheard of in India; this was a rare event (*New York Times*, December 12, 2007).

As you can see from the list of shootings that have been reported in the media, there is no shortage of stories to tell. What one can surmise from these stories is that each author gives the story his or her own twist. The press is very good at inventing great bylines to catch the reader's eye. The headlines are loaded with mystery or have a shock factor. People see the story and are drawn in to read by their curiosity. Journalism schools train their students well. They know that attraction is three-quarters of the battle to getting readership.

In reading many of these stories, the facts seem to change from day to day. It seems that several key facts had either previously been reported incorrectly or that there was new evidence discovered. Newspapers created new scenarios almost as fast as they could publish the stories. The sad part of journalism in this country is that so many people believe that newspapers are the gospel truth.

Many Americans do not have the ability to think critically about the issues and are very gullible. There are some very reliable and reputable media organizations that pride themselves on telling the truth as it truly is, not a fabricated version of what the truth needs to be, or should be, to sell newspapers. Print media is probably the easiest to regulate, as once it is printed, it is on record forever. Researchers can go back and look at archives of what was written and published. We have the ability to look with a much more critical eye, as history allows us to reexamine at our leisure. Television, on the other hand, is a beast of a different nature and color.

Television is fast-paced, immediate, and gone in a flash. Studying how television uses its ability to inform the masses proved to be much more of a challenge. Getting access to former news reports was much more time-consuming and tedious a job. The work of television is to bring it to you as it happens. There is very little time to sit back and reflect. It is onsite reporting. This is what makes it so intriguing and exciting to viewers.

Seeing a reporter at the scene telling a story can capture our attention, but also can produce a story full of reporting errors, conjectures, and even fabrication. These on-the-spot reports are what often fuel gossip or rumors that have not been substantiated, but they do make for great television. School shooting events are great fuel for reporters and news broadcast networks. They increase viewership as well as ratings.

People are glued to their television sets and become available to companies for marketing. Advertising wins when there are events like school shootings. Advertising capitalizes on viewers' fears and increases occur in the sale of firearms, security systems, or personal protection items. Everyone involved with the media wins. The only losers in all of this are the victims of the shootings. They are used to make great news coverage, to rally the community into action of some sort, and at times to effect changes in protocols and procedures, or increase the presence of law enforcement in a community.

In conclusion, we know the media is here to stay. We know they play a powerful role in the information we receive about events. We need to be able to trust that what they are feeding us is accurate and done in a professional manner. We have to demand that the media be accountable and responsible for the delivery of quality information at all times, and that they do not sensationalize it.

The goal of a media system is to inform. It is my hope that by being responsible and respectful we will see a change on how stories and events are reported. We as the people of this country deserve the best in skills from the ones who tell us what is going on in the world. We need them to be ethical. They need to demonstrate integrity and not sell their souls for the almighty dollar of selling newspapers or television ratings.

Honesty in the delivery of information is our right. We will expect nothing less. The victims and families of school shootings deserve to be respected and have their story told in a way that they can be remembered and honored. Everyone in this country deserves the right to be valued and have a sense of belonging.

The media must have these rights as their guiding force. They must accept the responsibility to do the best job possible at all times. All individuals who chose this career path must be willing to set a high level of professional and ethical standards to guide them as they do their job. They are the recorders of our history. How will people view this time in world history? They will look back at was written and televised. Are we leaving an excellent set of records that will truly show what these troubled times were like? I sure hope so.

13

Gangs: The Families of Crime

Gangs—defined as a group of people that form an allegiance for a common purpose and engage in unlawful or criminal activity—have been around for centuries. Gangs have been around in the United States since the Revolutionary War; for example, Jesse James and his gang are well documented.

Gangs are not a new phenomenon. They are having an enormous impact, as they can be found in all parts of the country. No geographical area, racial or cultural group, or school district is immune from the problems of gangs. Due to the increase in gang activity and interventions around existing gangs, communities must become proactive in trying to deal with this issue. It is a problem which families, schools, and communities must unite to solve.

Estimates of gang activity vary. The U.S. Department of Justice has estimated more than 16,000 gangs exist with more than 500,000 gang members, while the American Bar Association estimates 23,338 different gangs exist with a membership of 665,000. The two American cities with major gangs are Los Angeles and Chicago. In Los Angeles it is the Crips and Bloods. In Chicago it is the Disciple and El Rukn, Vice Lord, and Latin King. Other types of gangs exist according to race and ethnicity. Other groups can make up gangs according to where the person is, such as the Jamaican Posse, prison, motorcycles, or a neighborhood.

Where do these young people who are attracted to the gang life come from? It seems that many gang members come from a matriarchal environment. The member is usually male, a poor student, or a school dropout. Many come from lower-class communities, where they are not able to attain wealth and success through traditional ways. The gang culture offers an organizational structure that spells out rules concerning expected level of aggressive behavior and the status gained by adhering to these rules.

The family structure is a crucial factor in determining whether a youth will become gang involved. If there is poverty, alcoholism, drug addiction, chronic illnesses, or incarcerated family members, youth are put at greater risk. A youth who comes from a dysfunctional family is more likely to seek out gang membership as a way to belong and gain recognition and protection. Other factors linked to gang activity are delinquency, lower socioeconomic status, ethnic minority status and identity, and lack of influence by parents.

There are three major types of delinquent gang activity: (a) racket activities, (b) violent conflict, and (c) theft. There are two types of gangs, entrepreneurial and cultural. There is a direct correlation between the presence of gangs in and around schools and increases in school violence.

There are three general but distinct statuses of gang membership: (a) wannabes, youth aged nine to thirteen who aggressively seek roles and status in a gang; (b) gangbangers, youth aged thirteen to twenty-five and already accepted as a gang members (the core, or soldiers, constituting about 80 percent of the members); and (c) original gangsters, usually the founders, who are permanent members and are retired or semiretired from the activity.

It is interesting to note that this hierarchy is very well defined in terms of what is expected. Wannabes must prove themselves by the work they do as mules for the drug trade or violent acts to prove their worthiness. Many continue a life of crime and end up in prison at some time.

Gang members, because of their dysfunctional backgrounds, are very emotionally on edge. Many have been found to have sociopathic personality disorders and are able to distance their emotions from their crimes. Many of these young males use females as sex objects and usually treat them very badly. If a young girl has a troubled past she is more likely to be recruited for the gang's sexual use or be pimped out as a prostitute.

Gang members are overtly homophobic and will present themselves with a macho image to dismiss the insecurities they may have over their own masculinity. The following characteristics are present: (a) limited feelings of guilt, (b) few feelings of compassion or empathy for others, (c) behaviors dominated by egocentrism and satisfying their own goals, and (d) manipulation of others for immediate self-gratification (Yablonsky, 1997).

School shootings have been linked more to individuals than to large gangs. There have been instances where the individual shooter has been part of a gang and has shot an individual student or committed a crime against the school as a way to prove his loyalty or desire to be part of that particular gang. Schools can do a self-assessment of whether or not gang activity could be a factor in a possible attack or shooting.

The control of a gang activity on school campuses is critical. Gangs are infused into the social structure of a school before staff is fully aware of the problem. The National School Safety Center has developed the following gang assessment tool.

1. Do you have graffiti on or near your campus? (5 points)
2. Do you have crossed-out graffiti on or near your campus? (10)

3. Do your students wear colors, jewelry, clothing, or flash hand signals or display gang-related behavior? (10)
4. Are drugs available near your school? (5)
5. Has there been a significant increase in the number of physical confrontations or stare downs within the past twelve months in or around your school? (5)
6. Is there an increasing presence of weapons in your community? (10)
7. Are beepers, pagers, or cell phones used by your students? (10)
8. Have you had a drive-by shooting at or around your school? (15)
9. Have you had a display of weapons at or around your school? (10)
10. Is the truancy rate of your school increasing? (5)
11. Are there increasing numbers of racial incidents occurring in your community or school? (5)
12. Is there a history of gangs in your community? (10)
13. Is there an increasing presence of informal social groups with unusual names? (15)

Scoring: Each yes response gives a score, which when calculated may indicate an issue.
0–15: No significant gang problem.
20–40: An emerging gang problem.
45–60: A significant gang problem.
65 points or higher: An acute gang problem that requires urgent attention and intervention.

This instrument is widely used by many school districts to assess their environments. It should be used in a way that will lead to constructive discussion and action on the part of school officials and administrators.

There has been much debate in the United States about the increasing social fragmentation that is occurring. It seems we are dividing ourselves by ethnicity, religion, gender, sexual orientation, class, politics, and so on. Due to this separation there has been an increase in social conflict. It is no wonder that youths seek out social support, shared values, and a sense of family and acceptance provided by the gangs.

Schools are heavy recruiting sites for new gang members. Gangs are often the leading competitors with communities for the hearts and minds of young people. Peer pressure to join gangs can be extremely powerful and difficult to resist. Incentives for gang membership include recognition, peer status, social support, family tradition or history, and protection and perceived opportunity. Gang members have a low rate of participation in school activities. Rarely do gang members bond or identify with a significant adult at school.

Although gangs are believed to account for large increases in overall crime rates, the evidence is not clear. Most crimes by gangs were reported as violent homicide and other violent crimes were the number one and two. The majority of gang-related crime is not a consequence of drug dealing; it is more often related to status and territorial disputes with members of other gangs.

Prevention Strategies: Individual

Often violence and delinquency are considered problems to be addressed at the beginning of adolescence, but the seeds of juvenile violence and delinquency can be sown as early as the beginning of pregnancy. Prevention begins with a continuum of care that starts at the beginning of a child's life and continues through late adolescence. The U.S. Department of Education developed a guide titled the "Seeds of Help: Youth Violence: Prediction and Prevention," highlighting the following developmental stages and prevention of violence. These interventions have been shown to prevent a child from becoming an at-risk youth. This list of interventions is not effective for all children, but has shown remarkable benefits to the children who receive them.

Prenatal/Perinatal

1. Increased medical care reduces delinquency, child abuse, and neglect.
2. Increased home visits by nurses before and after birth decrease abuse and enhance parenting.

Birth to Age 4

1. Increased family and child bonding.
2. Increased parenting skills.
3. Increasing learning readiness.
4. Social skill development.
5. Increased behavior training decreases negative parenting.
6. Involvement in Head Start programs.

Ages 4–6

1. Learning readiness and social competence skill-building can help to develop early attachment to school as a positive experience and decrease the chances of academic failure.
2. Strategies such as small class size work well in kindergarten and first grade.
3. Promoting alternative thinking strategies reduces early antisocial behavior by integrating emotional, cognitive, and behavioral skill development.

Ages 7–12

1. Meaningful and challenging opportunities to contribute to family, school, peers, and community in de-

velopmentally appropriate ways to promote the development of life skills needed for adult roles.
2. Development of self-esteem.
3. Recognition of child efforts and self-worth.
4. Incentives to continue with positive activities.
5. Comprehensive neighborhood afterschool programs that create opportunities for community involvement and service (Boys and Girls Club of America).
6. Cooperative learning programs.
7. Homework clubs that allow students to work in teams to assess progress and prepare for tests.
8. Anger management and conflict resolution skills training.
9. Substance abuse prevention programs.
10. Family strengthening programs.
11. Tutoring.

Adolescence (Ages 13–18)

1. Continuing in-school positive peer models.
2. Opportunities for work experiences.
3. Cultural awareness programs.
4. Environmental work projects.
5. Job placements.
6. Afterschool activities.
7. Employment skill building.
8. Gang intervention.
9. Leadership skill training.
10. Vocational training.
11. Mentoring programs.
12. Recreation and sports programs.
13. Curfews.
14. Grassroots community coalitions that strengthen and mobilize communities.
15. Community partnerships (police, media, business, civic organizations, neighborhood crime watch, etc.).

16. Investment in economic, social, and physical infrastructure so opportunities exist for future employment for these youths.

To help youth not to join gangs and become criminals who take weapons to school and hurt other people, we need to be aware that creating positive opportunities for these youths starts very early, long before they make their way to school. If society becomes more diligent in implementing the strategies listed above, we will all benefit from the efforts that go into prevention and intervention.

Family Interventions

Family and parental involvement is the number one tool for fighting gang involvement. Strong families are a major asset. Parenting does matter, and the ethnic group one belongs to may have a big impact on which kids become gang members. Single-parent families can begin very early to instill in their children a sense of worth and respect for others and themselves.

There are many antigang programs that are successful with families. They are programs that provide more leisure time activities for youngsters, support tougher law enforcement against gang activities in the community, increase efforts to dry up sources of gang revenue, such as drugs, and increase parental supervision of children, including their activities and friends. Parents who become better parents become better fighters against gangs just by becoming more responsible for their children. Parents can do the following:

1. Monitor the company their children keep.
2. Monitor their children's whereabouts.
3. Keep their children busy with positive activities at school, church, or in organized recreational activities.
4. Model good behavior for their children and let them know how they are valued as individuals.

5. Spend time with their children and include them in family activities often.

6. Watch for signs of pre-gang activity and at the first sign intervene quickly and seek help from school, community groups, and law enforcement. Police officials are willing to help deter youth from gang involvement (McCarthy, 1998).

School Recommendations for Preventing and Intervening with Gangs

A prevention-intervention program strategy for gangs should be developed in close collaboration with parents, law enforcement officials, and the community at large. It is the responsibility of all to monitor young people in the community for any indicators of gang activity or presence. Gang symbols should not be allowed on a school campus. Formal programs should be in place to divert students from gang membership.

Strategies need to be in place for responding immediately to gang incidents that occur at schools. Law enforcement must be a key player with any intervention that involves criminal or violent activity. Model programs such as Rising Above Gangs and Drugs by Natalie Salazar and the National School Safety Center's Gangs in Schools are excellent resources for schools in developing gang prevention-intervention strategies. Below you will find a summary list of recommendations from these sources.

1. Begin gang prevention efforts as early as possible in a child's school career; some kindergarteners and first graders show clear signs of emerging gang involvement. Early intervention is more likely to divert children from later gang involvement. It is key to involve and support the parent on a variety of levels with multiple services and support.

2. Improve the social cohesion of neighborhoods and communities. Schools are important partners with families, police, churches, courts, corrections, and social service agencies in working toward this goal. It is important to create safe neighborhoods for all its residents.

3. Develop a comprehensive interagency system for sharing records and information to effectively address gang problems that will allow early intervention and guide prevention efforts. In this day and age with technology there is no reason for ignorance or lack of information sharing on both children and families.

4. Build the following three components into a gang prevention-intervention strategy: (a) a strong law enforcement component that allows detection and detention of chronic gang members, (b) an intervention component that controls gangs activity on school campuses and allows gang members to escape gang involvement, and (c) a prevention component to positively influence vulnerable children and youths who are on the cusp of gang activity.

5. Make strong, positive role models available at school.

6. Maintain sports programs.

7. Provide at-risk students with access to computers, labs, and instructors.

8. Provide afterschool recreation and leisure programs to students and their families.

9. Reinstate the teaching of morals and values and socially responsible decision-making in the school curriculum.

10. Expose students vulnerable to recruitment by and involvement in gangs to (a) adult and peer mentoring, (b) academic tutoring and support, (c) strategies to engage in the schooling process, (d) social skills training geared to building and maintain friendships, and (e) effective home and school communication and collaboration.

11. Develop a gang-prevention policy on campus with law enforcement officials.
12. Implement a gang-prevention curriculum.
13. Confront and remove all graffiti on school buildings within twelve hours.
14. Develop a comprehensive set of school strategies that include (a) clear behavioral expectations, (b) visible staff, (c) parent involvement, (d) in-service training, (e) graffiti removal, (f) cooperation with law officials, (g) existence of a gang-prevention plan, and (h) community involvement and coordination.

It is highly recommended that schools begin the discussion around these interventions to prevent gang activity and also to prevent the individual student who may be part of a group from acting out on his own or on the behalf of his gang. It is paramount that schools begin to address the factors listed above as part of their intervention programs. Not doing so is downright foolish and irresponsible on the part of school administrators.

In today's environment it is essential that schools have resources to consult as they begin to discuss the likelihood of a school tragedy and attempt to manage the crisis when it does happen. Below are a list of resources and guidelines.

Websites

"Early Warning Timely Responses: A Guide to Safe Schools," www.ed.gov/offices?OSERS/OSEP/Products/earlywrn.html.

The Gang Awareness Page, www.novagate.com/novasurf/gang.html.

Gangs or Us, www.gangsorus.com.

"Safeguarding Our Children: An Action Guide," www.ed.gov/offices/OSERS/OSEP/products/actionguide.

Skinhead Street Gangs, www.aracnet.com/~1wc123/skinhead.html.

Street Gang Dynamics, www.gangwar.com/dynamics.html.
Students Against Violence Everywhere, www.national
save.org.
U.S. Office of Juvenile Justice and Delinquency Prevention, www.ncjrs.org.
U.S. Office of Safe and Drug-Free Schools, www.ed.gov/
offices/OSDFS/index.html.
"What's a Parent to Do About Gangs?" www./ncpc.org/
10ad2.html.

Organizations

The National School Safety Center
Gang Crime Prevention Center
National Gang Crime Research Center
National Youth Gang Center
The influence gangs have in our society is felt by all in
many cities and towns. Gangs serve a purpose in our society.
Only when society, which includes individuals, schools, and
communities, unites to give all the possibility of opportunity
will we see the decline of gang membership. Gangs provide
acceptance, safety, and security. Only when all members feel
they can be part of mainstream society and get the American
Dream will we see fewer disadvantaged and dysfunctional
youth who feel the need to rob and kill other members of the
community.

It is key that communities come together to provide early
intervention and ongoing prevention activities, and have effective laws and enforcement and value all members of the
community if we are to see an increase in community pride
and progress. We have a long road ahead of us.

14

Personal Stories

This chapter is dedicated to the personal stories, poems, and experiences that children have had with bullying, harassment, and/or violence. Many of these stories come from school children and college students. Names have not been included at the request of the individuals. Many of the poems used in this book come from children's writing that was first written for a play about bullying at Plymouth State University. The TIGER Theatre Company graciously donated these stories to be used in this book to highlight what children have experienced and are experiencing. The author wishes to thank TIGER Theatre Company and all the children and individuals who contributed to this chapter.

Original writings collected by TIGER (Theatre Integrating Guidance, Education and Responsibility), a professional educational theatre company touring original musical productions based on children's writings about social issues facing young people in our schools today based at Plymouth State University, Plymouth, NH. For bookings contact (603)536-5227.

~

"Bullies"
The time to stand up to bullies is now.
But many kids don't know how.
They ruin children's lives, with every word they say.
And then go home thinking everything's okay.
I've never stood up to a bully before,
But whoever does should get an award.
Why these kids do it I don't know.
They could have something going on at home.
But just because they're feeling bad.
They shouldn't make others so sad and mad.
If I were a bully I would be scared.
I wouldn't even dare to make fun of someone else.
Because if they get too angry they may burn down your house!
Ruining lives should not be a sport.
They should be thinking of love and happiness of all sorts.

⚬—

I know I did right, but what will he do right?
He'll just beat me up worse, even get others in too.
He will inflict more pain and cause more sorrow,
So I'm scared to go to school tomorrow.
What I did that day was brave and wise,
Because the bully had apologized.
The counselor had told him my side of the story,
So we became friends; I had nothing to worry.
So I took a stand for what was right,
So when I get older I just might
Go to other places to help stop this war,
So it's not just me who's not bullied anymore.

⚬—

I'm at my desk, nervous, unwilling.
To leave the class when the bell will ring.
I tap my pencil, the tick-tack of the clock,
But time seems to stop, right when the bell rings.
The scuttle of people to hurry to class,
I felt home-free, but alas,
The presence of the bully at 5 foot ten.

Will break my spirit once again.
I conceal my face, but he noticed too soon,
He walks up to me to continue my doom.
He shoves my head in the locker door.
Just like he always did before.
No apology, no pity, no more than a shove,
I feel I'm below him; he feels he's above.
Just because he's older and stronger,
But I just can't take this bullying any longer.
I make a bold move, I'm scared, but I must.
So I start to head to the school's office.
I tell the counselor, he gets to the trouble,
But I know the pain from the bully will become double.

⌒

I think bullies need to know how it feels to be hurt by someone.
This is what I have to say to them.
Don't laugh at me, don't laugh at my glasses. I don't like one who
    harasses.
Don't call me names; I could be a famous singer with a wife,
When you are in jail for your entire life. I could be doing
Surgery on someone, doing an amputation when you are
A terrorist, blowing up the whole nation. I could be someone
Climbing from a helicopter on a rope when you are on 36th street
Selling your dope.
I could be a truck driver with a big rig, then you stop the jig.

⌒

I'm the kid out on the playground,
Whose always chosen last,
I'm the one who is made fun of,
'Cause all that matters is my past.
But you don't think it matters, how I really am.
I need special help in school, 'cause I can't work alone.
My clothes are always tattered,
And I haven't got a home.
But you walk through,
Like you're okay.
Always seem so good, 'cause no one will stand up to you,

The way they know they should.
You may have your problems of your own,
But to cause me more pain.
Now I am over the problem and feeling good.
So, if you have a problem see someone. You should understand
That problems only get worse if you don't take care of them.
Now anger should burst so play it sage
You really should
Because if you take care of it you will feel good.

~——

I'm a bully, I'm mean and I'm lean. Mess with me, and I'll make
  you scream!
My idea of fun is to make kids run, I can do it to you for a dollar
  or two!
People say, "Wow!" when I walk by just because I'm six feet high.
  I'm by
Far the best in my class—surely this year I will pass.
If you even try to talk or walk with me, I'll knock you to the
  ground just to show you I'm the best in the town!

~——

"I Sit Alone"
Kids play on the blacktop; I sit alone.
Friends play basketball; I sit alone.
They say they had too many people; I sit alone.
They let others join; I sit alone.
I have glasses; I sit alone.

~——

"Bullies"
I wish they could see
How it feels to be me.
How every day you could be scared
Of what seems to be,
Bullies.
No one enjoys being picked on.
And some think they can't go on.

If this is the way life will be,
Then I only wish that they could see
What it's like to be bullied.

⌒

"Bullies"
Why?
Why do they do that?
I don't know.
Are they angry at me,
Or are they jealous?
I don't know.
And what did I do to them?
Nothing at all.
They make me feel upset and angry.
I didn't do anything to deserve it.
And why do they laugh?
It's not very funny.
Picking on other kids is just wrong.
There's no future in that.
Maybe if they know how it feels,
They would stop.
Knowing that there is someone watching your every move
Is not very fun.
Having to watch your every move
Is not very fun.

⌒

"Bullies on Our Minds"
Hi, I'm a kid that gets picked on,
Turn around once and I'll try to be gone.
Nothing I can do can turn away,
From ruining a perfectly good day.
They think they're tough and really cool,
But they have me swimming in a hatred pool.
I'll never feel the same about them,
They'll never make me feel like a gem.
I hate the way they treat me.

They make me feel like a small little pea.
I hope you don't turn out like me,
Bullied, small and certainly not free.

◦—

I go to school everyday
While other kids run and play
I just hope I don't get hurt
'Cause everyday I get treated like dirt
I get teased and pushed around
They may not care or know
But yesterday they broke my nose
Every night I go home all banged up
Sometimes it's not just my body that gets hurt
Sometimes it's just my heart
They never seem to stop
Everyday seems the same
I just hope that tomorrow will be different
Until that day I will just keep on hoping
That tomorrow they will stop the teasing and joking

◦—

"Sticks and Stones"
Hurtful words are always heard,
But are they taken seriously?
Loser,
Freak,
Wanna-be,
But do they listen?
Yes,
They do.
A poke,
A punch
Or even a kick,
It isn't a joke from their point of view;
They take it seriously,
Physically and mentally,
How mentally?
Maybe they think they are worthless,

Or that they deserve to get beat up,
Guess what?
They don't.
Physically there is a bruise where they were hit,
But if you hurt them enough,
There will be a mark that you leave,
Not on their skin,
But in their mind.
Do they deserve to be made fun of?
No,
They don't,
So Stop,
You're ruining their lives.

~

"The Bully"
I come to school and I stay in fear, for he will soon be here.
I creep along the lockers, he pounces down the hall.
I want to leave, but that would be against the law,
And I know that he will find me; he knows where I go.
He waits for me outside.
In sadness I go.
He torments me and hurts me.
But why I do not know.
There must be a reason why he loves to depress me so.
Maybe it's his own insecurity that it might be so.
I don't know why he chose me, but one day he did.
Maybe if he knew me, he wouldn't make my days a dread.

~

"Why Me?"
As I walk down the halls of the school, I get hit with people's
    backpacks.
They say, "Move it, fag!" I get out of the way. It keeps happening.
By the time I get to the end of the hall, I feel about three inches tall.
    Quickly, I duck into class, hoping, just hoping the bullying stops
    at the end of school.
But then I realize the bus is still ahead.
I and sit down and hide. "People are not nice," I think to myself.

The bullying starts again on the bus this time. When it's over, it is
    my stop.
So I walk down the alley and I say to myself, "Why me?"
When kids attack,
In ways we can and cannot explain or understand,
Physically and emotionally, others get abused.
Kids hurt physically,
Stuffing in lockers,
Pushing in halls,
Hitting without reason.
You can't feel all abuse on your body—
Insults in looks,
Exclusion from groups
General ignoring
Kids who bully don't just hurt the abused's life;
They hurt their own,
Inflicting emotional abuse on themselves,
Every time an insult passes their lips.
It's not always their fault; parents are sometimes to blame.
Some parents don't realize how much a boy is until it is too late.
They neglect, ignore and promote violence.
All this pain leads back to them.
Kids who are bullied don't express their feelings of hate,
They don't tell the person his/her life will be sad.
Don't tell them that while I suffer now,
My life will be much better.
People think bullies are a bad few,
Whose parents didn't listen,
Whose personality was mean,
Who wanted attention.
But everyone is a bully at some point
Human nature dictates
Weaker opponents who won't fight back are easier targets,
Than ones who will stand up for themselves.
The differences is,
When good people bully, their good friends tell them,
And they come to their senses.
They apologize,

Take back a statement.
Sometimes an apology
Can be the difference between friendships and enemies.
If someone has a different opinion,
Different feeling,
Different personality,
They are likely suspected to be excluded.
People who are different,
Pose a threat to the leaders,
People following will keep them atop their platforms of leadership.
People different can divert the followers and topple them.
The followers, usually not as mean as the leaders,
Still have a conscience,
Wanting to help the needs
But they like their spot.
Following makes them fit in,
Makes them happy,
And stable.
Too much of the leader comes off on the followers;
They get ideas.
Why would they risk this great place of happiness and comfort,
For the happiness and comfort of reject.
Not everyone is like this, though;
There are people who defy regularity,
Become friends with "unpopular":
These friends will help them.
The leaders, however,
Their fate is sealed,
They have no friends, just followers,
The road ahead looks dark.
So this is to people who are the victims of this horrible act,
People who are used to the threats and insults,
People who think there is no light at the end of the tunnel.
There is,
And before you know it, your future and life will start to brighten,
Your world of peace and understanding will arrive,
And you will truly be happy.

⌒

"Into The Mind of a Bully"

There are an infinite number of reasons why kids bully other kids, and every single one of those can be remedied. The reasons are there and almost always the reason is something that is so common, yet so infantile. Sometimes it is out of ignorance or lack of knowledge. Someone might bully someone because of a birth defect or handicap that, in truth, really could not be helped or avoided because that's just the way things are. Often times people bully others because of the way they were raised. Maybe they had bad parents or weren't taught respect or moral behavior when they were growing up. On that same note, bullies were almost always being bullied at some point whether it was by a parent or someone at school. However, by far the most common reason that someone would be bullied is the fact that they're just different. For example, one day in gym class we were playing hockey. The way we play at our school is the teacher lays all the sticks out, and then he selects a group of people and tells them to go get a stick. He does not pick teams, so it is possible to have all the good people on one team. It's not really fair, but hockey isn't really taught much anyway.

Now, there is a kid in our gym class who gets made fun of all the time. He is from a different country and he speaks English well, but not great. Now a few kids came up with this idea, they went and told our foreign friend, let's call him Joseph, that he should get a red stick because they are all going to get one. Joseph happily agrees to their seemingly nice offer. So, when the call comes to get sticks Joseph scurries right out and grabs a red stick and when he looks up there's a smile on his face bigger than Texas. What happened after that gave me an empty feeling in the pit of my stomach. As he looked up he saw the sneering faces of his so-called teammates. They were all standing there laughing with their blue sticks in hand. The look on Joseph's face would have brought rain from the sky. He knew what happened and he felt so betrayed because he had placed his trust in them and they had stomped on it in a disgusting way.

Now if I were a bully the look on Joseph's face would be enough to keep me from ever doing as much as throwing someone a dirty look. He was so embarrassed and let down that he started laughing too, just to try and make it look like he didn't care. You could tell, though from the look in his eyes that he didn't think it was funny. He looked like his mother had just been murdered. I don't know what would bring someone to do this. Probably, like I said before, just ignorance and the inability to accept someone different. When you think about it, it really is just stupid and childish, but unfortunately, that's just the way bullies are.

⌒

A lot of people, kids and adults alike, bully others, but refuse to believe that what they're really doing is considered bullying. I have the firsthand experiences on both sides, some that happened long ago and others more recent. The feeling one gets when being picked on is like no other, but it is always the same, a mixture of embarrassment, self-hatred, depression, and just wondering what you ever did to that person because no one, good or evil, of any sex, religion, race or creed, deserves to be treated that way. A lot of adults say bullies just pick on others because they feel bad about themselves, but most of the time it's just to inflict damage on others, treating them the same way someone treated or treats you. Deep down in everyone where your conscience is, you feel a pang of guilt and sympathy whenever you hurt someone purposefully. But the real bullies are the ones that make countless remarks about your unchangeable features, actions, or just digging down to your deepest self and feelings, and making you think that everything about you is wrong.

Those bullies have no conscience whatsoever, because if they did, they'd realize how heartless and just plain cruel they were really being and the worst part is that these people are often your friends, or so-called friends, who take advantage of your feelings and the friendship itself. Thinking you need them more than they need you, and just pushing you to the boiling point until you can't help or control anything. These bullies sincerely need a taste of their own medicine, or military camp to straighten them and their heartless feelings out. But the sad thing is, nothing can be done about bullying because no matter how much you tell an adult they never really seem to get it. They forget that they were probably in the same position when they were a kid, looking down while harsh remarks and criticism came their way like bullets. Waiting to pierce the feelings of those seemingly weaker than them.

The worst part is when one does not stand up for the person, and continuously lets it continue, in fear of the comments that might come their way. But I guess that's a real test of friendship, whether this "friend" would stand up for them, or look away until it was over. And that's right there, that's the meanest thing to do, as mean as what the bully's doing, turning your back on someone when they truly need you. It's wishful thinking to think everyone could be like that, sticking up for their friends, no matter who, when you are being verbally attacked by someone. It would sure make it a lot easier to have someone right by your side, telling the bully off, and never thinking of themselves, but of you. That's the only thing that would matter, not the hurtful words, or even the beating up, but the faithfulness of a real, true-blue friend.

∽

Just because I don't dress, act, or look cool doesn't mean I'm not. I've seen many kids do stupid things to be cool. But not me; I will not embarrass myself just to be "cool." I am not rich and my hair is horrible. You don't think I already know that but I do. You don't think I can hear you behind me in science, but I can. Also, you don't think I dress good enough, look good enough, or act cool enough. But to myself and others, I do. If you don't like me, okay, but don't make fun of me so no one else will like me. Everything you find "wrong" about me I already know because you taunt me and tease and embarrass me in front of my friends so that I will have no friends. I may not seem cool, but oh well, don't make life harder or I just might make yours worse. I don't want to, but if you push, I am afraid to push back.

◦—

If I was in that position, I would say, "Why do you bully people, huh? Give me one good reason why you bully . . . I think I know, you are jealous of us because we have good friends and we are smaller. If you would just be yourself and be nice you might be surprised what happens, if you came to school nice, I would have been your friend. It's better than not having friends. You're also jealous because we know how to be nice and know how to get people to be our friends. So if I were you, I would think about what I just said and you may have more friends and have a happier life."

◦—

If you like to be a bully, you should feel how it feels to be hurt by someone. Bullies aren't any better than anyone else in the school or out of the school. You are not the handsomest guy or the prettiest girls anyways. You might think you're really tough, but believe me, you are not. There's someone in this world that could say some pretty nasty things about you so you should think twice before you say something.

◦—

I think bullies need to know how it feels to be pushed around, or punched, or kicked. I would be so happy when a bully would meet his match and lose, so he can feel how the ground tastes after he gets punched in the face. And maybe if he found out the other side of a fight, he might stop bullying other kids, and maybe, just maybe, the kids who were being bullied, after seeing the bully be beat, might stand up to the bully. Then he would stop. There are some bullies in my school and when they meet their match they are usually big wimps about it.

⌁

Why do you think some kids bully other kids?
What do you think is going on in their minds?
I think some kids bully other kids because they get bullied at their house or maybe they are insecure about themselves so they take their anger out on somebody else. I sometimes see bullies picking on other kids and it looks like they are unhappy with themselves. Sometimes people bully other people because they think they are better than them or they have more control than them. But that is usually only when someone is older than one another. I remember one time this kid Harold was calling my friend Bertha names. For instance he was saying, "Moron," "Butthead," "idiot," "Bertha you big tub of lard," and "you big fat cow." I felt really bad for her because she was trying to ignore him but it was kind of impossible because he kept following her around and saying those things really loud so everybody could hear him. He actually never physically touched her but it hurt her just as bad when he was saying those mean things to her.

⌁

"Getting to the Point!"

I was behind the door watching a kid with plain clothes on cowering in front of two kids. One of the kids looked a little unsure of himself. The other had a smirk on his face. They were both dressed in baggy pants and a shirt. They were making fun of the other person. The onlooker did not know what to do. I think some mean kids, also known as bullies, bully people because of the way they look, act, talk, and even if they're smart. I don't bully people because I don't want to be bullied.

Victim: Why are these kids doing this to me? Why don't they just leave me alone? I never did anything to them. What did I do to deserve this? Why are they calling me names and why are they bullying me?

Unsure Bully: I really don't want to make fun of this person. My friends will laugh at me if I don't. I really want to fit in.

Bully: This person is dressed in un-cool clothing. Why shouldn't I pick on him? I am bigger than he is, too.

Onlooker: I think I should help. What if he starts to bully me? But I really want to help. Maybe I'll go tell. What if he calls me a tattle tail? I better just walk away and pretend I didn't see anything. I hope they did not see me.

These are some different point of views in which people might think in this situation.

∾

"The Shape of a Bully"
The shape of a bully, is no certain shape,
The anger they have, they just let escape,
By hurting innocent children, who have done nothing wrong.
The size of a bully is neither big, nor small.
A bully isn't either short or tall.
The race of a bully,
Isn't always the same,
But the anger they cast upon you is awfully lame.

∾

A bully is mean,
A bully is seen,
But not on a picture, or movie screen.
Bullies are bad,
They make people mad, and sad, but bullying is certainly
Not a fad.
It has been here forever,
And will leave, never.
And lashes you whenever!
It's quite a scare,

So be aware.
A bully is there!
Here in Hampstead Middle School,
Bullying isn't cool.
It's just not fair,
But hardly rare,
They are just inescapable; it's always there.
The bullies don't care
They laugh and they stare,
They point and they snare.
The point we must make,
Is that bullies aren't fake.
They are here,
They are there,
They are everywhere.
There is no certain shape,
There is no certain size,
There is *no* certain race,
There is *no* certain face.

~

"I Have a Dream"

I have a dream that one day our schools will be better. Kids will not make fun of each other and beat them up, or care how much money they have or what clothes they wear. We need the schools to spend a little money to fix the water fountains, lockers and also clean up the bathrooms and fix the front sign. All these things will make our school more appealing and become a better place to learn.

I dream that people will not be so full of hatred and will stop destroying the things I mentioned previously. That the city would clean up the place they call a school playground on the side of the building. Students slide on the ice and fight because there is nothing else to do. Fixing the basketball hoops and the usage of basketballs may improve the misbehaving.

Maybe they could also improve on the food we eat at school; for example, ask us what kinds of salad dressings we like, or give us sour cream for our tacos. Just little things like this can make huge improvements!

Finally, that maybe the lunchroom teacher and support staff could handle problems among students better. When someone reports something, they should look into it before it escalates.

⟳

Dear . . .

I wanted to let you know how special you are to me. You are my Identical Twin Brother and my best friend. Mom calls us the "Dynamic Duo." We are there for each other. I think it's fun to hang out with you. We have fun playing hockey and basketball games. It's really cool to snowboard with you! Camping with "sis" and mom and dad is awesome! I love to check out the creek for crawfish with you, and hike Gunstock Mountain together. I like to watch you complete in Special Olympics and help out too. You're my brother and it is cool. At night, when Mom and Dad tuck us in to bed and kiss us goodnight, you sneak down from the top bunk and sleep in my bunk. We like the same games and the same colors. We share our sentences and friends. Sometimes we dress alike and sometimes we don't. Sometimes we like each other and something's we fight. That's ok, you're my brother and I love you always. I am proud of you. You have Cerebral Palsy and walk with a brace. In schools, you have a tutor for help and when the teacher tells you, you wear your glasses. That's okay, it's you and you're pretty cool! You never complain, and always try much harder at everything. Mom has always said, "Your disability is not an inability." You know it!

Sometimes, I know you are hurt and being bullied. I hear other kids call you "leg problem boy" or "retard." I see bully's having a bad day pick on you, because it's easy. In the lunchroom one day, a girl placed a sticker on your back with a loser sign. On the bus, sometimes they pick on you, because you walk different. One day I saw a kid from the neighborhood punch you and kick you because he lost a scrimmage game. Mom was mad, but you just cried and walked away. And it's not just kids. Sometimes I head adults say, "He has issues." What issues? Don't they know, everyone is different and everyone has feelings? I don't see the issues. I've seen you cry when you come off the bus sometimes. Some days, it's not so easy, but Mom says, "Not to give them credit and walk away even when it's hard to." It's okay to feel sad when you're hurt by others. People who judge others are not secure with themselves. We were always told to believe in ourselves and you do. You are my big brother and best friend. I am very proud of you. You have shown others, it's okay to have a disability even when it's hard. We are the "Dynamic Duo" always. Just be you and I'll be me.

"An Innocent Victim"

An innocent victim is hurt. I see it every day. But do you really observe what's going on? What do I do to stop it? Do I even try?

Today I was in the lunch line and I saw a wretched thing. A kid pushed another person to the dusty and dingy floorboards just to get ahead of the poor kid in line. I stood in line in front of these immature kids, watching as an innocent bystander. In my heart I knew that I had to tell someone, but on the outside I knew that if I did I might be that kid on the floor. I watched the unfortunate kid slowly getting up and trying with the utmost of effort to hide his tears. They were there, and they will never go away.

Another place where I saw an awful thing happen is in the girls' locker rooms. There are many acts of bullying here because there is no supervision. An innocent girl was horribly made fun of because she changed in a stall. Again I wanted to tell an authority figure. I thought if there was just a way that I could tell someone without anyone else knowing. I was dreadfully confused. I did not know what to do. One half of me wanted to take charge and help this poor girl, but the other half of me wanted to just hide and go along with everybody.

People today think that if someone does something different or is different, they deserve to be made fun of. Everybody is different in one way or another. I know my school strives to stop bullying, but it is going to take a lot of time and effort to fix this terrible dilemma.

⌒

College Students

These stories were written by college students in an education teacher preparation program at Plymouth State University in New Hampshire.

⌒

Back when I was in 2nd grade, I had a horrible teacher. She was very scary and I feel like she never liked me. I remember throughout my 2nd grade year I never missed a day at school because I was so terrified at what my teacher would say. Though my teacher was never physically abusive towards me or any other student, I feel as if she was very emotionally abusive. I recall a time when I was at recess and I had been playing on the monkey bars. Suddenly I was surrounded by a group of boys who were trying to look up my skirt (since it was a picture day and I was dressed up). As I tried to quietly get away from the boys, I moved across the monkey bars and accidentally kicked a boy in the face. The boy immediately dropped to the ground and all of his friends didn't look very happy. So I ran to a teacher to protect me. But, this teacher was my very scary 2nd grade teacher who absolutely loved the boy who I kicked in the face. She proceeded to accuse me of doing everything on purpose and made me sit in time out all day and think at what I had done. By the end of the day when it was time to go home, she had proceeded to write a horrible note to my parents that explained my behavior. So as I walked home, I was so scared as to who my parents would believe. But thankfully they believed me. She then proceeded to make my papers wrong, failing me on numerous occasions. Soon my parents were forced to make an appointment to take with her and the principal. I remember being there for the meeting, but I was walking around the classroom, not at the desk with my parents, teacher, and principal. The teacher finally confessed that she had been being "hard" on me and said that she was sorry. The principal felt horrible about what I had gone through and closely watched me throughout the rest of the year, as well as my parents. But I still am terrified of that one teacher who for some reason despised me and wanted to do everything in her power to make sure I suffered. Thank goodness for my parents and the principal who saved me from being held back in her class. I could never imagine what that would have done for me.

This all took place where I was in 2nd grade in the year of 1993. I would rather not disclosure the name it where it happened. We'll just say it was in NH, because like I said, I am still afraid of her.

⟋⟍

The most violent episode I encountered was in high school. I was a sophomore at a small private school. We sat down for lunch in our dining hall—all grades eat together. A teacher approached a senior whose name was Jeff. She asked the student to take off his hat, school rules. He started talking back to her, then his anger skyrocketed he started pushing tables over and then he jumped out of a nearby window. Jeff had scrapes all over, but because the dining hall is on the first floor that was it. An ambulance and police car arrived minutes later. For those five minutes the male teachers were trying to restrain the student until he calmed down, which he did as soon as he got into the ambulance. He later received help and was required to take anger management classes and to come back after a mandatory suspension. He chose not to return to our school. I think embarrassment played a role in that.

⌒

When I attended High School at Kennett Jr. Sr. High School in Conway, NH, violence was not an issue until I became a senior in 1997. Violence usually occurred between two boys, but the incident I am going to talk about involved two girls. These two girls were both juniors, while I was a senior. I remember walking to one of my classes when this incident happened. I believe the incident occurred half way through the school year.

The hallways were crowded during the transition from one class to another and you only got three minutes. I believe I was already in my English class, waiting for the bell to ring, when "Maria" and "Jenny" had their altercation. Most of the time girls just pulled hair and slapped one another, but not these girls. I believe that "Maria" was making derogatory statements about "Jenny" to one of her friends, not realizing that "Jenny" was walking behind her. Now "Maria" was only liked by a few people and "Jenny" was known throughout the High School as a fighter and did not like "Maria" for personal reasons. "Maria" had her way with the boys and I believe she was being flirtatious with "Jenny's" boyfriend throughout the school year.

Anyway, "Jenny" heard "Maria" talking and all of a sudden, "Jenny" pushed "Maria" up against some lockers. People were still trying to get to class at this time, so innocent bystanders got shoved as well. "Maria" tried to punch "Jenny," but she was too quick for her. Instead, "Jenny" knocked

"Maria" to the floor and then they were punching, kicking, and slapping one another. "Jenny" ended up on top of "Maria" with her hands around her throat. By now, everybody was watching the fight. "Jenny" was still on top of "Maria" and clutching her throat when she pulled out a knife. She had the knife to "Maria's" throat and that is when the principal and Resource Officer got involved. They had to pull "Jenny" off of "Maria" and while this was happening, "Jenny" was still threatening "Maria."

Both of the girls got suspended. Most of the student talked about the fight for the rest of the day considering this happened around 10:00 a.m. Since "Maria" had such a shady reputation, most of the girls said they would have done the same thing if they were in the same situation that "Jenny" was with her. "Maria" was not well liked by the girls of the school at all. I think after each one got suspended, "Jenny" returned to school, but I believe that "Maria" was home schooled for the remainder of the year. She ended up being talked about for the rest of the year, even though she was not physically present at school.

This fight happened more than ten years ago and I can still remember the look of fright on "Maria's" face and the look of pure hatred on "Jenny's" face. Each girl had personal problems as well, so I am sure the fight was heightened by this. A few people were cheering "Jenny" on, but I feel that at that time, neither one of the girls were listening to the crowd, but were anticipating what the other's next move was going to be. I do not remember being scared, just nervous. I always get nervous when I see fights.

Today, each girl is a mother and both still live in the North Conway area. Once they were seniors, the Resource Officer was full-time at the school, so I do not think there were more altercations between them ever again. Violence and drugs became issues, but these two girls were not part of the problem ever again.

⌒

In my class I was always quiet and shy. I noticed more things than anyone. One day we got a transfer student whose name was Joey. I knew the second he corrected the teacher of his name that he was bad news. After class I talked to my friend about the new student. She mentioned she got a new student too and his name was Billy. They ended up being twins. The twins would come into school smelling horrible and until they pulled out a dead rabbit their backpack out. That is when we knew why. Every day the twins would fight, scream, yell and cause problems. Many windows and school property were broken because of them until one day they just disappeared.

⌒

I was not like the rest of my classmates at the Manchester School of Technology, therefore, they felt the need to make my life miserable by constantly bullying me. At the time, I was a junior in high school, who spent a third of my stay at MST studying culinary arts and then I would go back to Central High for my regular classes. I had to beg, plea and argue with my mother to allow me to go to MST. I wanted to study culinary arts. Mom had always felt that I was "better" than the other students that were going there. MST is a voc-tech school, and I had already been taking college prep courses, so therefore it must mean I was college bound.

My classmates were always talking about smoking pot, drinking alcohol and having sex. I would not participate in those discussions but talk about my experiences as a cake decorator and my desires to go off to college. One morning, while on the school bus to MST, a classmate pulled out a bag of weed and offered it to me for free. I was disgusted at him and refused his offer. My life at MST would forever change after this moment.

The bullying first started out with verbal harassment. The kids assumed because I wasn't talking about having sex, that I must be a lesbian. I found myself crying in class all the time, because I was trying to defend my sexuality. It hurt me so much that they were saying horrible things to me, even though I am straight, as I have many wonderful gay friends. The verbal harassment would soon change to physical. At some point, a couple of the guys starting hitting me. They even went as far as taking a spray bottle with bleach and ruined my favorite blue shirt that had a beautiful butterfly on it.

My teacher was well aware of what was going on. I would cry to her. She would talk to the class. Things would be quiet for a couple of days. Than the bullying would start again. I would cry to her again. She would talk to the class again. The bullying would cease for a day or two. After several weeks of this, I decided I couldn't handle it.

One morning, I did not get on the bus to go to MST, but I ran to my guidance counselor's office bursting in tears. I begged her to change my class schedule. I didn't want any more of my clothes that I bought with my own money ruined. I did not want to be called a lesbian. I didn't want to be touched while I was trying to learn about culinary arts. The innocence in my desire to learn about baking diminished. I no longer wanted to go back to school.

My guidance counselor called the principal of MST. He had a discussion with the entire class about bullying. My class schedule was completely altered which presented a huge inconvenience, as I had wonderful friends in my other classes. I did go back to MST, but during another part of the day.

As a teacher, I will be sensitive to the atmosphere of my students. I understand the emotional pain of what it is like to be attacked on a daily basis. My teacher is in no way to blame for what happened as she wasn't the one speaking or hurting me. However, I always felt she didn't intervene enough. I can't say I am necessarily glad that this experience occurred, but it will make me a stronger teacher.

⌒

In my high school, there were the typical boy fights and girl fights. The two that were fighting were surrounded by a crowd chanting and raving. Once there was a fight between the rednecks and so-called gangsters and punks. The police had to come and break that up, or at least that was the rumor.

When my little brother was in second grade, there was a young boy named Stephen in his class. Stephen came from a tough family background. He threatened to bring his hand gun to school and shoot everyone in the class.

My little brother, when he was in 4th grade, was cut by a third grader on the bus. The third grader cut him with a plastic knife.

⌒

In my eight grade class, two boys had had some trouble before, but someone did something wrong. One kid threw a stool right at the other kid's head. The kid who had the stool thrown at his head was knocked out for a few seconds. This all happened during class.

⌒

These stories and poems only confirm that violence, harassment, bullying and intimidation are alive and well in our schools today. Many children suffer in silence and going to school is an exercise in survival. How can school officials become more aware and stop these behaviors? It will only stop once all members of the school community become empowered to use and teach respect and citizenship to the children in their care. It begins with one bully, one victim and one adult. It can be a war we win.

15

Resources: There Is Help After All!

In this chapter you will find many resources throughout the United States. These resources are a beginning point in your search for help. The author does not endorse one agency or program over another but presents these for information purposes only.

Antiviolence Hotlines and Nationwide Resources

National Domestic Violence Hotline

Phone: (800) 799-7233
Hotline available twenty-four hours a day, seven days a week.

American Bar Association Commission on Domestic Violence

Address: 740 15th Street, NW, 9th Floor, Washington, DC 20005-1022
Phone: (202) 262-1000
Website: www.abanet.org/domviol/home.html

The American Bar Association Commission on Domestic Violence website provides information about a wide range of domestic violence issues and extensive links to other resources and organizations. The website includes listings of ABA policies, training materials, legal briefs, and sample legal forms relevant to domestic violence issues and proceedings.

Asian Task Force Against Domestic Violence

Address: P.O. Box 120108, Boston, MA 02112
Hotline: (617) 338-2355/Phone: (617) 338-2350/Fax: (617) 338-2354
E-mail: asiandv@atask.org
Website: www.atask.org
Based in Boston, the mission of the Asian Task Force Against Domestic Violence is to eliminate family violence and to strengthen Asian families and communities. Many of their brochures are available in Hindi, Japanese, Khmer, Korean, and Vietnamese.

AYUDA, Inc.

Address: 1707 Kalorama Road, NW, Washington, DC 20009
Phone: (202) 387-4848
Website: www.ayudainc.org
A Washington, D.C., organization, AYUDA is Washington, D.C.'s leading source of multilingual legal and social assistance for low-income Latinos and foreign-born persons in immigration, human trafficking, domestic violence, and family law.

Break the Cycle

Address: 5200 W. Century Boulevard, Suite 300, Los Angeles, CA 90045
Phone: (310) 286-3366/Fax: (310) 286-3386
Website: www.breakthecycle.org

With offices in Los Angeles and Washington, D.C., Break the Cycle is a national nonprofit organization that engages, educates, and empowers youth to build lives and communities free from dating and domestic violence. Break the Cycle provides youth with preventive education, free legal services and information and peer leadership opportunities. Founded in 1996, Break the Cycle serves as a national resource and advocate on the issue of teen dating violence. Through innovative partnerships with schools, universities, social service providers, law enforcement, community groups, law firms, and corporations, Break the Cycle provides youth with tools to break the cycle of dating and domestic violence.

Boys Town

Phone: (800) 448-3000
Website: www.girlsandboystown.org/home.asp
Help at the end of the line. Anyone, anytime, any day. Or visit the Quick Tips section to read about issues that deal with suicide worries and taking on tough problems.

BWJP Criminal Justice Office

Address: The Criminal Justice Center, 2104 Fourth Avenue South, Suite B, Minneapolis, MN 55404
Phone (toll free): (800) 903-0111, ext. 1/Phone: (612) 824-8768/Fax: (612) 824-8965
E-mail: technicalassistance@bwjp.org
Website: www.bwjp.org
BWJP's Criminal Justice Office offers training, technical assistance, and consultation on the most promising practices of the criminal justice system in addressing domestic violence. Criminal Justice staff can provide information and analyses on effective policing, prosecuting, sentencing, and monitoring of domestic violence offenders.

BWJP Civil Justice Office

Address: 1601 Connecticut Avenue NW, Suite 500, Washington, DC 20009

Phone (toll free): (800) 903-0111, ext. 1/Phone: (202) 265-0967, ext. 130

The BWJP Civil Office provides important leadership aimed at enhancing justice for battered women and their children in the civil legal arena by improving battered women's access to civil justice options and quality legal representation in civil court processes. This office typically provides technical assistance on such issues as: protection orders; separation violence; divorce and support; custody; mediation; confidentiality of shelter records and lay advocate testimony; safety planning; and welfare and the Violence Against Women Act.

Corporate Alliance to End Partner Violence

Address: 2416 East Washington Street, Suite E, Bloomington, IL 61704

Phone: (309) 664-0667/Fax: (309) 664-0747

E-mail: caepv@caepv.org

Website: www.caepv.org

The Corporate Alliance to End Partner Violence is a national nonprofit organization dedicated to reducing the costs and consequences of partner violence at work—and eliminating it altogether. From policies and programs to legal issues and legislation, CAEPV is a source for information, materials, and advice.

Department of Justice Office on Violence Against Women

Address: 800 K Street, NW, Suite 920, Washington, DC 20530

Phone: (202) 307-6026/Fax: (202) 307-3911/TTY: (202) 307-2277

Website: www.usdoj.gov/ovw

The mission of the Office on Violence Against Women (OVW) is to provide federal leadership to reduce violence against women, and to administer justice for and strengthen services to all victims of domestic violence, dating violence, sexual assault, and stalking. This is accomplished by developing and supporting the capacity of state, local, tribal, and nonprofit entities involved in responding to violence against women.

FaithTrust Institute

Address: 2400 North 45th Street #10, Seattle, WA 98103
Phone: (206) 634-1903/Fax: (206) 634-0115
E-mail: info@faithtrustinstitute.org
Website: www.faithtrustinstitute.org

FaithTrust Institute, formerly the Center for Prevention of Sexual and Domestic Violence, is an international, multifaith organization that offers a wide range of services and resources, including training, consultation, and educational materials, to provide communities and advocates with the tools and knowledge they need to address religious and cultural issues related to abuse.

Family Violence Prevention Fund

Address: 383 Rhode Island Street, Suite 304, San Francisco, CA 94103- 5113
Phone: (415) 252-8900/Fax: (415) 252-8991
E-mail: info@endabuse.org
Website: www.endabuse.org

The Family Violence Prevention Fund (FVPF) works out of offices in Washington, D.C., San Francisco, and Boston, to prevent violence within the home, and in the community, to help those whose lives are devastated by violence because everyone has the right to live free of violence.

Generation Five

Address: 3288 21st Street #171, San Francisco, CA 94110
Phone: (415) 861-6658/Fax: (415) 861-6659
E-mail: info@generationfive.org
Website: www.generationfive.org

The mission of Generation Five is to end the sexual abuse of children within five generations. Through survivor leadership, community organizing, and public action, Generation Five works to interrupt and mend the intergenerational impact of child sexual abuse on individuals, families, and communities. Rather than perpetuate the isolation of this issue, Generation Five integrates child sexual abuse prevention into social movements targeting family violence, economic oppression, and gender and cultural discrimination. Generation Five collaborates with other organizations to ensure that accessible, culturally relevant services are available to both survivors of child sexual assault and offenders.

Kids Help

Phone: (800) 668-6868
Website: www.kidshelpphone.ca/en/

Information, tips, links and more that you can use in facing life's challenges. Canada's only toll-free, twenty-four hour, bilingual and anonymous phone counseling, referral, and Internet service for children and youth. Every day, professional counselors provide immediate, caring support to young people in urban and rural communities across the country.

Miles Foundation

Address: P.O. Box 423, Newtown, CT 06470-0423
Phone: (203) 270-7861
E-mail: Milesfdn@aol.com or milesfd@yahoo.com

Website: members.aol.com/_ht_a/milesfdn/myhomepage
The Miles Foundation is a private, nonprofit organization providing comprehensive services to victims of violence associated with the military: furnishing professional education and training to civilian community-based service providers and military personnel; conducting research; serving as a resource center for policymakers, advocates, journalists, scholars, researchers, and students; and serving to ensure that public policy is well-informed and constructive. The Foundation is responsible for the development of a coalition of organizations throughout the country and abroad fostering administrative and legislative initiatives to improve the military response. The Foundation and its partners drafted "Improving the US Armed Forces Response to Violence Against Women: Recommendations for Change" (copies of this document can be requested by contacting the Foundation via e-mail or phone).

National Coalition Against Domestic Violence

Address: 1120 Lincoln Street, Suite 1603, Denver, CO 80203
Phone: (303) 839-1852
E-mail: mainoffice@ncadv.org
Website: www.ncadv.org
The NCADV is the oldest national organization representing grassroots organizations and individuals working to assist and empower battered women and their children. It serves as a national information and referral center for the general public, the media, battered women and children, agencies, and organizations. They offer shelters and support services for battered women and their children.

National Domestic Violence Hotline

Phone: (800) 799-7233/TTY: (800) 787-3224
Website: www.ndvh.org

A project of the Texas Council on Family Violence, the National Domestic Violence Hotline is open year-round. Trained staff provide counseling and referral services to all, free of charge. The staff speaks English and Spanish, and translators are available for 129 other languages. They offer crisis intervention, referrals to domestic violence and other emergency shelters and programs, information and support, and can link callers to a nationwide database on domestic violence. They advise on shelters, advocacy and assistance, and social services programs. They also run the National Youth Crisis Hotline at (800) 448-HOPE.

National Online Resource Center on Violence Against Women

(A project of the Pennsylvania Coalition Against Domestic Violence and the National Resource Center on Domestic Violence)

Address: 6400 Flank Drive, Suite 1300, Harrisburg, PA 17112-2778

Phone: (800) 537-2238/TTY: (800) 553-2508/Fax: (717) 545-9456

Website: www.vawnet.org

The National Online Resource Center on Violence Against Women (VAWnet) is a comprehensive online resource for advocates working to end domestic violence, sexual assault, and other violence in the lives of women and their children.

Pace Women's Justice Center

Phone: (914) 422-4069

Website: www.law.pace.edu/wjc

E-mail: jbavero@law.pace.edu

The Pace Women's Justice Center is a training, resource, and direct legal services center comprised of Pace law students and faculty, attorneys, and advocates dedicated to eradicating domestic violence and furthering the legal rights of women through skillful and innovative use of the law. The Center's goal is to give those who support battered women, the elderly, women with low income, and victims of sexual assault the legal tools they need to stop violence against women, seek economic justice, protect families, and save lives. The Center also publishes a newsletter on the legal system and domestic violence.

Pennsylvania Coalition Against Domestic Violence

Address: 6400 Flank Drive, Suite 1300, Harrisburg, PA 17112

Phone: (800) 537-2238/TTY: (800) 553-2508/Fax: (717) 671-8149

Website: www.pcadv.org

PCADV, a private nonprofit organization, is proud to have been the first state domestic violence coalition in the country. At the national level, PCADV operates the National Resource Center on Domestic Violence, the National Online Resource Center on Violence Against Women (VAWnet), and the Women of Color Network (WOCN).

Rape, Abuse, and Incest National Network (RAINN)

Address: 2000 L Street NW, Suite 406, Washington, DC 20003

Phone: (202) 544-1034/Hotline: (800) 656-4673 ext. 3

E-mail: info@rainn.org

Website: www.rainn.org

Provides information on resources throughout the country, for survivors of rape, abuse, and incest. Runs a twenty-four hour, seven-day-a-week hotline.

Safe Horizon

Address: 2 Lafayette Street, 3rd floor, New York, NY 10007

Phone: (212) 577.7700

Fax: (212) 577.3897

Website: www.safehorizon.org

Based in New York City, Safe Horizon is the largest provider of domestic violence services in the country. Collaborating with the criminal justice system, Safe Horizon offers innovative programs that provide women with support throughout the complex process of leaving violent relationships and building safe futures. For survivors of domestic violence, stalking, rape, and sexual assault, Safe Horizon offers services that help them and their children move toward safe and independent violence-free lives.

SAFER: Students Active for Ending Rape

Address: 25 Washington St, Suite 411, Brooklyn, NY 11201
Phone: (347) 293-0953
Website: www.safercampus.org
SAFER provides organizing training and support to college and university students so that they can win improvements to their schools' sexual assault prevention and response activities. By offering students the necessary support and resources, confidence-building and leadership training, SAFER empowers student activists to rally the community and push school administrations to take action.

SAGE (Standing Against Global Exploitation)

Address: The SAGE Project, Inc., 1385 Mission Street, Suite 300, San Francisco, CA 94103
Phone: (415) 905-5050/Fax: (415) 554-9981
Website: www.sagesf.org
The Standing Against Global Exploitation Project—or the SAGE Project—is a nonprofit organization with one primary aim: bringing an end to the commercial sexual exploitation of children and adults (CSE/CSEC). We at SAGE contribute to that goal by raising awareness about CSE/CSEC issues, and by providing outreach and services to CSE/CSEC survivors. SAGE services are nonjudgmental and holistic, assisting pros-

titutes and sex workers in an organized, professional, and compassionate manner that doesn't further traumatize the persons seeking assistance.

Sanctuary for Families

Address: P.O. Box 1406, Wall Street Station, New York, NY 10268-1406
Phone: (212) 349-6009
Website: www.sanctuaryforfamilies.org
Sanctuary is a nationally recognized domestic violence agency that provides a range of culturally sensitive and integrated services. Sanctuary provides crisis intervention, emergency and transitional housing, individual and group counseling, job readiness and mentoring programs. Through its legal center, they offer legal advice and direct representation, mentor volunteer attorneys, and advocate legal reform.

UNIFEM

Address: United Nations Development Fund for Women, 304 East 45th Street, 15th floor, New York, NY 10017
Phone: (212) 906-6400/Fax: (212) 906-6705
E-mail: unifem@undp.org
Website: www.unifem.org
UNIFEM is the women's division of the UN and the website has information about responses to violence against women around the world. UNIFEM provides financial and technical assistance to innovative programs and strategies that promote women's human rights, political participation, and economic security. Within the UN system, UNIFEM promotes gender equality and links women's issues and concerns to national, regional, and global agendas by fostering collaboration and providing technical expertise on gender mainstreaming and women's empowerment strategies.

V-DAY

Website: www.vday.org

V-Day is a global movement to stop violence against women and girls. V-Day is a catalyst that promotes creative events to increase awareness, raise money, and revitalize the spirit of existing antiviolence organizations. V-Day generates broader attention for the fight to stop violence against women and girls, including rape, battery, incest, female genital mutilation (FGM), and sexual slavery. V-Day is also a nonprofit corporation that distributes funds to grassroots, national, and international organizations and programs that work to stop violence against women and girls. The "V" in V-Day stands for victory, valentine, and vagina.

Women's Law Project

Address: 125 S. 9th Street, Suite 300, Philadelphia, PA 19107

Phone: (215) 928-9801/Fax: (215) 928-9848

E-mail: info@womenslawproject.org

Website: www.womenslawproject.org

Based in Philadelphia and Pittsburgh, Pennsylvania, the Women's Law Project provides phone counseling and legal information to callers, on any aspect of law that touches women's lives, including domestic violence, and especially regarding reproductive rights.

WomensLaw.org

Address: 150 Court Street, 2nd floor, Brooklyn, NY 11201

Website: www.womenslaw.org

WomensLaw.org was founded in February 2000 by a group of lawyers, teachers, activists, and web designers interested in seeing the power of the Internet work for more disadvantaged people and specifically for survivors of domestic violence. WomensLaw.org changed its formal name from the

Women's Law Initiative in 2005. The mission of Womens Law.org is to provide easy-to-understand legal information and resources to women living with or escaping domestic violence. By reaching out through the Internet, they empower women and girls to lead independent and productive lives, free from abuse.

Resources for Young People

Break the Cycle

Phone: (888) 988-TEEN

Break the Cycle is a 501(c)(3) nonprofit organization whose mission is to end domestic violence by working proactively with youth. Break the Cycle provides domestic violence prevention and early intervention services to youth aged twelve to twenty-two through three programs: the Education and Outreach Program (conducting outreach, presentations and training for youth, teachers, school counselors and officials, law enforcement personnel, parents and social service providers); the Legal Services Program (providing early intervention services, including free legal advice, counsel and representation, to hundreds of young people each year, assisting them to escape abusive relationships or homes); and the Peer Leadership Program.

The Empower Program

Website: www.empowered.org

The Empower Program is an innovative and effective program that works with youth to end gender-based violence. Through partnerships with schools and local organizations, Empower develops and teaches programs that give young people the skills and strategies to prevent violence in their own lives, and encourages them to take an active role in ending the culture of violence.

A Family Guide to Keeping Youth Mentally Healthy and Drug Free

Phone: (800) 789-2647 (mental health)/(800)729-6686 (substance abuse)

Website: family.samhsa.gov

This website from the Substance Abuse and Mental Health Services Administration (SAMHSA) was developed to support the efforts of parents and other caring adults to promote mental health and prevent unhealthy activities among seven- to eighteen-year-olds. It is a great resource for information on date rape drugs.

Feeling Safe: What Girls Say

Phone: (800) GSUSA4U

Website: www.girlscouts.org/research/publications/original/feeling_safe.asp

This links to the executive summary of *Feeling Safe: What Girls Say*—an original research study by the Girl Scouts of the USA (GSUSA), in partnership with Harris Interactive, Inc.—a national (online and focus group) study of over two thousand girls aged eight to seventeen conducted in an effort to better understand how girls perceive safety. Researchers sought answers to such questions as . . . How safe do girls feel? What are the negative effects of girls feeling unsafe? How important are emotional and physical safety to girls? How can adults make girls feel safe?

4 Girls Health

Website: www.4girls.gov, www.4girls.gov/bullying/index.htm

This website, developed by the Office on Women's Health in the Department of Health and Human Services, gives girls between the ages of ten and sixteen reliable, current health information. The site focuses on many health topics that respond to adolescent girls' health concerns and motivates girls to choose healthy behaviors using positive, supportive, and nonthreatening messages.

GirlsAllowed

Website: www.girlsallowed.org/Home/home.aspx
An animated web site for girls eleven to fourteen, designed to engage girls as "allowed" (welcome) and "aloud" (having a voice) with a focus on helping girls develop positive attitudes about themselves and build a foundation for healthy relationships and healthy living. The site focuses on helping girls learn to identify healthy and unhealthy relationships before becoming involved in potentially abusive ones—and to help girls become active in intimate partner violence prevention in their communities. GirlsAllowed is a program of the Corporate Alliance to End Partner Violence. (Winner of the 2003 SXSW Web Award—Grrl Category).

Girls Incorporated National Resource Center

Address: 120 Wall Street, New York, NY
Phone: (800) 374-4475
Website: www.girlsinc.org/
The Girls Incorporated website provides research, advocacy information, and tips on issues surrounding girls and young women. Girls Incorporated is a national nonprofit youth organization dedicated to inspiring all girls to be strong, smart, and bold. With roots dating to 1864, Girls Inc. has provided vital educational programs to millions of American girls, particularly those in high-risk, underserved areas. Today, innovative programs help girls confront subtle societal messages about their value and potential, and prepare them to lead successful, independent, and fulfilling lives.

Girl Power!

Website: www.girlpower.gov

A multiphase, national public education program sponsored by the U.S. Department of Health and Human Services to help encourage nine- to fourteen-year-old girls to make the most of their lives. Their strategy is to bring the issues of teenage pregnancy, prostitution, suicide, and poor health to the mainstream, to advocate institutional changes and to directly work with girls to develop their self-esteem and self-reliance skills so they may become healthy independent adults.

Family Violence Prevention Fund

Address: 383 Rhode Island Street, Suite 304, San Francisco, CA 94103

Phone: (415) 252-8900/Fax: (415) 252-8991

Website: www.endabuse.org

"In Their Own Words: Teens Speak Out"—endabuse.org/programs/children/files/prevention/TeensSpeakOut.pdf—was created by the Family Violence Prevention Fund as a result of their conversations with eighty teens across the United States regarding their thoughts about violence in the home and on the street.

National Center on Domestic and Sexual Violence

Address: 316 West 12th Street, Suite 109, Attn: Gail Parr, JD, Treasurer, Austin, TX 78701

Website: www.ncdsv.org/publications_dateteenviolence .html

Keep Safe Stay Cool

Website: www.softcon.com.au/kssc

Keep Safe Stay Cool is an early intervention program targeting young people between the ages of thirteen and twenty-five, using a peer education model to promote healthy relationships as opposed to domestic violence.

Los Angeles Commission on Assaults against Women in Touch with Teens Program

Website: www.lacaaw.org/itwt.html

The website provides information on counseling, hotlines, and programs. The In Touch With Teens Program is an innovative new curriculum that teaches twelve- to nineteen-year-olds how to build violence-free relationships.

Love Doesn't Have to Hurt—TEENS

Website: www.apa.org/pi/cyf/teen.pdf

This site, developed by The American Psychological Association with consultation from the Partners in Program Planning In Adolescent Health (PIPPAH), contains helpful information for teens about healthy and unhealthy relationships, how to identify both, and suggestions on how to make changes if you are in an unhealthy situation.

Love Is Not Abuse

Website: www.loveisnotabuse.com

A Liz Claiborne site with great information for adults, parents, and teens, including free downloadable handbooks, and a special dating violence web site. The site would be a great link for a company intranet, since the information would be valuable for employees and for their children!

Mentors in Violence Prevention (MVP)

Website: www.sportinsociety.org/mvp/

The Mentors in Violence Prevention (MVP) Program, founded in 1993 by Northeastern University's Center for the

Study of Sport in Society (CSSS), is a leadership program that motivates student-athletes and student leaders to play a central role in solving problems that have historically been considered "women's issues": rape, battering, and sexual harassment.

National Youth Violence Prevention Resource Center

Phone: (866) 723-3968 (866-SAFEYOUTH)

Developed by the Centers for Disease Control and Prevention and other federal partners, the Resource Center provides current information developed by federal agencies and the private sector pertaining to youth violence. A gateway for professionals, parents, youth, and other interested individuals, the Resource Center offers the latest tools to facilitate discussion with children, to resolve conflicts nonviolently, to stop bullying, to prevent teen suicide, and to end violence committed by and against young people. Resources include fact sheets, best practices documents, funding and conference announcements, statistics, research bulletins, surveillance reports, and profiles of promising programs.

National Domestic Violence Hotline

Phone: (800) 799-SAFE

If someone is experiencing domestic violence call the National Domestic Violence hotline.

Reachoutnh.com

Website: www.reachoutnh.com

This website for teens is a joint effort by the New Hampshire Coalition Against Domestic Violence and the New Hampshire Governor's Commission on Domestic and Sexual Violence. The site contains information on domestic violence, stalking, sexual assault, how to reach out to a friend, public service announcements, and more.

Report-it.com

Website: www.report-it.com

An early warning detection and intervention system created to prevent school violence by empowering students to speak out via an anonymous, secure, online "hotline" that alerts school officials to potentially dangerous situations.

SeeItandStopIt.org

Website: www.seeitandstopit.org/pages/

This is a website created by teens in Massachusetts to help other teens take a stand against relationship violence. It includes a gallery of print, radio, and TV ads.

Teen Action Campaign

Address: c/o The Family Violence Prevention Fund, 383 Rhode Island Street, Suite 304, San Francisco, CA 94103

Phone: (415) 252-8900/Fax: (415) 252-8991

E-mail: info@teenactioncampaign.org

Take Care Online

Website: www.takecareonline.org

This site (now in English and Spanish) aspires to help young people recognize and avoid unsafe relationships, and provides access to free information about healthy relationships.

TEENpcar.com

Website: www.teenpcar.com/default.asp

Based upon PCAR's (Pennsylvania Coalition Against Rape) teen sexual violence prevention campaign, this site allows visitors to listen to clips from the Xpose CD, read excerpts of the *TEENesteem* magazine, test their knowledge of sexual violence, learn what to do if victimized, and find out how to advocate for change.

Teen Relationships Website

Phone: (800) 300-1080
Website: www.teenrelationships.org
Covers such topics as abuse and respect, and offers help to teens seeking support, assistance, information, counseling, shelter, and other services via their twenty-four-hour hotline. "VolunTEENS" facilitate a chat room and answer hotline calls. Teen Relationships is a site for teens about dating violence, recognizing warning signs for an abusive relationship, understanding what a healthy relationship is, and resources for teens in abusive relationships.

Teen Victim Project

Phone: (800) 448-4663
This website is sponsored by the National Center for Victims of Crime. It contains information on topics such as bullying, assault, dating violence, robbery, and more. It is available in English and Spanish.

UHaveTheRight.net

Website: www.uhavetheright.net/
"U Have the Right [to a Healthy Relationship]." This site, sponsored by Verizon Wireless, provides a list of characteristics of both healthy and unhealthy relationships, a test to find out if your relationships are healthy, information on what to do if you or someone you know is in an unhealthy relationship, and domestic violence resources for adults and teens, including organizations, and books for teens and parents.

School Emergency Supplies and "Go Kits"

Every school, before and after care center, and day care center should store emergency supplies in preparation for either an evacuation or an emergency that requires students and staff to shelter in place. The safety team should select supplies that address the needs of the specific school, its population, climate, facilities, and resources. Because emergency supplies are so important, the school safety plan should reference both the supplies to be stockpiled and staff role responsible for stocking and replenishing.

"Go Kits"

In case of an emergency evacuation, it is critical that every classroom and the administration maintain a "go kit," a self-contained and portable stockpile of emergency supplies, often placed in a backpack and left in a readily accessible but secure location so that it is ready to "go." The school safety plan should reference the go kits and not the personnel to whom responsibility is delegated for sticking and replenishing them. The contents of the go kits should

Table 15.1.   Go Kit Items for Consideration

Administration go kit supplies	Classroom go kit supplies
Clipboard with	Clipboard with
List of students	List of students
List of students with special needs and description of needs (i.e., medical issues, prescription medicines, dietary needs), marked *confidential*	List of students with special needs and description of needs (i.e., medical issues, prescription medicines, dietary needs), marked *confidential*
List of school emergency procedures	List of school emergency procedures
Whistle and hat for leadership identification	Whistle and hat for leadership identification
Battery-operated flashlight	First aid kit with instructions
Utility turnoff procedures	Student activities (such as playing cards, checkers, inflatable ball)
Emergency communication device	
First aid kit with instructions	

reflect the safety team's consideration of the school's circumstances and resources.

School Emergency Supplies

Every school should store emergency supplies in case its students and staff required to shelter in place due to an emergency or a lockdown. All supplies should be securely stored in an accessible, central location. They should be labeled, protected, and maintained. Supplies that have expiration dates (such as batteries, food, water, and prescription medications) must be replenished over time. The safety team leadership should delegate the responsibility for making sure that these kits are properly stocked and replenished.

Schools should consider the following lists in light of their particular needs. Some items are easily stored while others are not. For example, extra clothing for young students is commonly stored in the classroom; older students could store extra clothes in their lockers.

Additional items that schools may want to consider include: radio equipment, emergency communication mechanisms, battery chargers, cigarette lighter cords, two extra 3A fuses, gas, and LED lanterns.

Schools may wish to coordinate plans for emergency clothing and sleeping supplies with the American Red Cross or another agency responsible for mass care in a crisis situation. In many situations the school will already be designated as an emergency shelter with plans already place for storage of cots and blankets.

Stockpiling personal prescription medications is complicated by many factors, including expiration dates, insurance, expense of extra doses, and temporary versus long-term needs. Schools may be able to arrange to have on hand more "routine" medications like insulin or epinephrine that could be kept in a first aid kit. Some medications will already be stored in the school for the chronic use of individuals. This is

Table 15.2. Supply Items for Consideration

Administration Supplies List	Classroom Supplies List	Student and Staff Supplies List
Designed command post with student roster (and photos), emergency contact information, and staff roster (with photos) in the form of a sign in/sign out sheet.	Clipboard with list of classroom students (and photos)	Jacket, raincoat
	List of students with special needs and description of needs (i.e., medical issues, prescription medicines, dietary needs), marked *confidential*	Change of clothes
Reflective vests or other means of identifying safety team members		Hat, gloves, and scarf where applicable
Whistles	List of emergency procedures	Food
Small directory with emergency telephone numbers of local drugstores, etc.	Whistle & hat (or other identifier) for teacher	Water
Walkie-talkies	Fist aid and supplies	Personal prescription medications where applicable
Pens, pencils, or wax numbers	First aid instruction manual	
Change for payphones	Medical gloves	
Special needs roster	Food	
Campus layout maps with evacuation sites, first aid sites, and parent reunification site	Water	
	Battery-powered flashlight	
First aid supplies	Batteries	
First aid instruction manual	Blankets	
Medical gloves	Bucket	
Food	Sanitary items (towelettes & toilet paper)	
Water supply	Work gloves	
Battery-operated flashlight or light sticks	Breathing masks	
	Plastic sheeting	
Extra batteries	Duct tape	
Battery-operated radio	Can opener	
	Hard candies	
	Student activities	

(*continued*)

Table 15.2. (*continued*)

Blankets
Portable toilets,
    makeshift toilets, or
garage bags
Sanitary items
    (toilet paper and
    towelettes)
Work gloves
Plastic sheeting
Breathing masks
Can opener
Waterproof matches
    and container
Lighter
Multipurpose tool,
    wrench or pliers,
    and knife
Speaker or megaphone
Utility turnoff
    procedures

Source: VMC®/Homeland Security Programs.
www.vmc.wvu.edu/CrisisWeb/PlanningTools/EmergencySupplies_n_GoKit101705.pdf.

an issue that must, at least, be discussed with parents, the school nurse, and the administrator.

Additional Information and Resources

Recommended Emergency Supplies for Schools

Website: www.redcross.org

The American Red Cross's website contains information on how and where to store emergency supplies and how much to stockpile. It also includes recommended supply lists for individual kits, an individual classroom, and an entire school.

*Practical Information on Crisis Planning for
Schools and Communities*

Website: www.ed.gov/admins/lead/safety/emergency
plan/crisisplanning.pdf

Developed by the U.S. Department of Education's Office
of Safe and Drug Free Schools, the guide offers particularly
useful information for schools assembling emergency supplies and classroom kits (see pages 6-25 to 6-27).

FEMA: Are You Ready?

Website: www.fema.gov/areyouready/

Offers advice for families and individuals on creating
kits for the home and at work. Much of the information is
transferable to schools and their preparedness efforts. It offers guidance for choosing as well as storing and maintaining items.

Supply Checklists

Website: www.ready.gov

Presented by Ready America (U.S. Department of Homeland Security), these checklists include supplies for such basic
needs as food, clean air, and first aid. Special checklists are also
available for portable kits and for people with special needs.

Emergency Management for Schools: Key Resources

Office of Safe and Drug-Free Schools Emergency Planning Website

Website: www.ed.gov/emergencyplan

Emergency planning is part of the department's Lead and
Manage My School series, a group of websites designed to

support administrators. It offers emergency planning resources, grants, publications, and more.

Readiness and Emergency Management for Schools (REMS) Technical Assistance (TA) Center

Website: rems.ed.gov

The REMS TA Center Website offers additional school-
based resources addressing emergency management through
its four phases. Resources include three major publications series, archived training materials, referral links, and the opportunity to pose direct technical assistance questions.

Practical Information on Crisis Planning: A Guide for Communities and Schools

Phone: (877) 433-7827

E-mail: edpubs@inet.ed.gov

Website: www.ed.gov/admins/lead/safety/emergency
plan/crisisplanning.pdf

The U.S. Department of Education has developed this guide
(publication ID ED003416P) to provide schools and their communities with a general introduction to emergency management as it applies to schools and basic guidelines for developing
school emergency management as it applies to schools and basic guidelines for developing school emergency management
plans based on the four phases of emergency management.

The Safe School Initiative

Phone: (877) 433-7827

E-mail: edpubs@inrt.ed.gov.

Website: www.ed.gov/admins/lead/safety/training/
responding/crisis_pg34.html

The U.S. Department of Education and the U.S. Secret Service collaborated to produce two reports and an interactive

CD-ROM that outline a process for identifying, assessing, and managing students who may pose a threat of targeted violence in schools, as well as provide ideas for creating safe school climates.

1. *Threat Assessment in Schools: A Guide to Managing Threatening Situations and to Creating Safe School Climates.*
2. *Final Report and Findings of the Safe School Initiative: Implications for the Prevention of School Attacks in the United States,*
3. *Safe School and Threat Assessment Experience: Scenarios Exploring the Findings of the Safe School Initiative* (interactive CD-ROM).

Tips for Helping Students Recovering From Traumatic Events

Website: www.ed.gov/parents/academic/help/recovering/index.html

This brochure provides practical information for parents and students who are coping with the aftermath of a natural disaster, as well as teachers, coaches, school administrators, and others who are helping those affected.

School Preparedness Virtual Town Hall

Website: www.vodium.com/goto/dhs/schoolprep.asp

The Department of Homeland Security and the Department of Education hosted a virtual town hall on K–12 school preparedness to provide an overview of grant opportunities, planning, training, and other preparedness tools available to school districts nationwide.

Epilogue

School violence—is it the wave of the future or is there a change on the horizon? Schools have become safer every year. It seems that every time we have a disaster we learn something new and develop new interventions. We have learned from previous situations that school shooters are individuals who are suffering internally and externally. Many of them harbor demons that manifest themselves in terms of severe mental illness.

We have seen many of these individuals act out in a time of emotional chaos or when they have stopped taking their medications regularly. Some have acted out on a moment's notice while others have planned the school shooting for years. The level of response to environmental, sociological, emotional, and psychological factors is so diverse that it is very difficult to develop an accurate measure or assessment that will reliably predict the possibility of a school shooting.

That the United States has the highest level of school shootings worldwide speaks volumes about what we believe about the possession of handguns and the right to bear arms. Is it time to reevaluate gun control? Is that the answer? Many educators think it is. Take away the guns and there will be no school shootings. But it is a bit naive to think that determined individuals will not be able to procure guns for themselves. They can and will find the weapons they need to carry out their mission.

Several gun violence researchers believe that an electronic lock in the grip of firearms would allow a gun to be fired by a person wearing a special decoder ring and not by unauthorized youth or children. These researchers believe that redesigning guns to reduce the number of bullets fired before reloading would decrease the number of deaths. Gun control in America always faces stiff political opposition. America must realize that it is time for change. If we look at the tobacco industry, we see it took years and almost two generations for people to recognize that smoking leads to health problems. The increase in lawsuits from the families of school shooting victims may accelerate the process towards better handgun control.

It is wonderful to see that more than 80 percent of our schools in America have a formal violence prevention or reduction program, but why is it not closer to 100 percent? School safety comes in many forms—installing metal detectors and security cameras, arming administrators and teachers, and lock-down procedures—but are schools really thinking about their protocols and procedures and practicing them with some level of fidelity?

Although we know that school shootings fluctuate in numbers, we also are aware of the increase in other areas of concerns regarding children and their development. Children are living in more poverty in this day and age then they have in a long time. They are lacking the basics in both physical and emotional needs.

Parents are becoming increasingly concerned about the anger that their children carry with them on a daily basis. Parents are able to see that their children lack the necessary coping strategies to effectively problem-solve and communicate their needs and wants. Parents need to pay attention to the interests and fantasies of their children. They have to monitor what their children is reading, what they are searching on the Internet, who their friends are, whether or not their children are involved with violent peers, and if the child is isolated or quiet and withdraws within their own world. Parents have to become aware of their child's artwork, writing, or music compositions.

The two-parent family structure is important in giving boys, especially, a good role model of responsible men. Many boys involved in school shootings were not involved with a significant adult male in their lives.

Young males today have not learned the value of work and sacrifice. They have not developed a sense of moral standards and interpersonal empathy. The groups of young men who have killed have been self-centered, very self-absorbed, angry youngsters who derive extraordinary pleasure from the savage revenge they wreak on other people.

They believe the world revolves around them. They are frustrated and in pain psychologically. They are not getting everything they want. They feel like victims. They have no concerns about others. To them, everything is about who they are and what they want. Many of these youths turn aggressive because they lack the ability to communicate, to negotiate, and to ask for what they want or need.

Physical aggression has occurred in human societies since we lived in caves. We have that instinctive behavior built into our brains. Fighting for survival is different from fighting for control, revenge, attention, and power. What has made aggression so interesting today is that guns have become the power symbol for many. It is the way to get what you want immediately. There are no lines, and no waiting is required.

School shootings create headlines. Many people are fascinated by the violence, secretly intrigued by the individual who pulls the trigger. They want to know what makes this person go crazy, and if it is something that they may experience as well. Though the days of the Wild West ended over a hundred years ago, a similar mentality still prevails in many parts of this country.

People still believe that they must protect their home and family at all cost, so guns must be present. If by chance someone stains your name or challenges your honor you need to be able to defend yourself. You must eradicate the other person or hurt him badly so that he will not come at you again. Children learn this message early on and adhere to it long after they have left their homes.

Media does play a role in enhancing kids' perspectives on mortality. Cartoons and movies show a character killed one week and returning the next. Kids grow up with a lack of understanding that life is transient. Since they spend up to six hours a day in front of the television, we know that this form of communication is a powerful influence on the development of both cognitive and emotional skills as well as coping skills.

The tragedies of school shootings raise issues that our society has grappled with for a long time. There has been a long discussion about finding the proper balance between providing for the safety and security of our communities while protecting and helping people with mental health illnesses get the care they need.

Several local, state, and federal government reports, task forces, and congressional and Senate committees have spent an enormous amount of time trying to find solutions that will make school shootings a phenomenon of the past. Several emerging themes have surfaced in multiple reports.

The first is that critical information-sharing faces substantial obstacles in the way it is procured or delivered in this country. Education officials, healthcare providers, law enforcement personnel, and others are not fully informed about critical information on persons who are likely to be a danger to self or others, and the resulting confusion does not lead to effective information sharing. States often do not communicate with federal or local agencies; the information is kept in isolation and not made available. Only once an incident has occurred do officials put all the pieces together.

The second theme is that accurate and complete information on individuals prohibited from possessing firearms is essential so we can know when an individual is seeking to acquire a weapon. State laws and practices do not uniformly ensure that information on persons restricted from possessing firearms has been duly recorded in the National Instant Criminal Background Check System.

Many families possess guns that are not recorded or licensed. Prospective school shooters do not need to go any farther than their own living rooms or garages to get the weapons they need. There has to be a better system to track weapons. This system must track weapons bought online as well and through local gun dealers. A better system of taking and keeping inventory is needed to overhaul the present system. We know that the present system does not prevent individuals who are mentally ill from acquiring guns. We just need to look at the Virginia Tech shooting and the Northern Illinois University shooting to know that both of those individuals had mental health issues, but were both able to acquire handguns locally.

The third theme is that there needs to be improved awareness and communication. These are the keys to prevention. To ensure the safety of our communities it is important that parents, students, and teachers learn to recognize warning signs and encourage those who are manifesting specific problems or behaviors to get the help and care they need.

Educators need to be aware of all the red flags and the physical, emotional, and psychological warning signs discussed earlier in this book. Professional development training needs to be offered to schools and districts on how to become more proactive in dealing with children and youths with emotional and behavior disorders.

The fourth theme is that it is critical to get people with mental illness the services they need. Meeting the challenge of adequate and appropriate community integration of people with mental illness requires a coordination of community service providers who are sensitive to the interests of safety, privacy, and providing valuable services that will lead to proper treatment and diagnosis. Early intervention is paramount to preventing acting-out behaviors in youths later in life.

The fifth theme is that we have had experience over the years with school shootings. We know what to do, but we have to be better at doing it. Many states and communities have already developed and adopted crisis and emergency plans and formulated excellent prevention plans to address school violence. Now the challenge is to fully implement these programs in the local community school and ensure that effective communication occurs; everyone must be on the same page as to what needs to be done and when. A plan is only as good as the people who develop and execute it.

The issue of school shootings is a complex one. In a country of over three hundred million it is impossible to eliminate all risks. America is a free and open society, so offices, malls, schools, sporting events, and so on, could all be potential targets at some point in time. The goal for most agencies and organizations is to minimize the possibility that situations could occur in the future.

There is no one-size-fits-all answer for all possible targets and communities in this country. It is impossible to predict where and under what circumstances a school shooting could occur. The context can range from a university setting to an elementary school, middle school, secondary school, and from a rural to an urban area. The threat can be from within or without. The key is to be prepared and vigilant and to know that it could happen anywhere and at any time.

The federal government has drafted up several recommendations: The U.S. Departments of Health and Human Services and Education will develop additional guides on how information can be shared legally under HIPAA and FERPA and disseminate it widely to the many education and law enforcement communities.

The U.S. Department of Education should ensure that school officials understand how and when postsecondary institutions can share information with parents. These departments need further actions to balance more appropriately the interests of safety, privacy, and treatment of students according to existing HIPAA and FERPA regulations.

Federal agencies should continue to work together and with states and appropriate partners to implement and coordinate and disseminate information and best practices in behavioral analysis, threat assessment, and preparedness for all educational institutions.

The U.S. Department of Education in collaboration with the U.S. Secret Service explores research of targeted violence in educational institutions and continues to share existing assessment methodology with interested institutions.

The U.S. Department of Justice, through the FBI and ATF, should reiterate the scope and requirements of gun laws, the use of the background checking system, and proper monitoring of these systems.

The U.S. Department of Health and Human Services helps schools and institutions develop cultures that promote safety and open communication and create environments conducive to seeking help and developing culturally appropriate messages to destigmatize mental illness and mental health treatment.

Training must be provided for parents, teachers, and students to recognize warning signs and known indicators of violence and mental illness and to alert those who can provide for safety and treatment.

A mechanism to report and respond to reported threats of violence must be established and publicized.

Mental health screening, treatment, and referral with primary health care must be integrated.

States and local communities should review emergency services and commitment laws to ensure the standards are clear and appropriate and that they strike a proper balance of liberty and safety for all in the community.

The Department of Homeland Security and Justice should consider expanding grant programs to be developed for additional training in behavioral analysis and active shooter training. There should be an emphasis on the detection of hazards through information sharing and grants should be made available for schools and organizations to develop their preparedness and prevention plans.

This is but a short list of recommendations that the federal government has enacted as a way to meet the challenge of school shootings. Are these the correct strategies or not? I believe that this is an excellent start toward effecting change on a large scale. America is a large, open space. To live freely we must be prepared to have certain risks in life. The goal of any program or intervention is to make sure that when it is needed it will work. Educators nationwide are paying attention and are including crisis response management practices in their daily instruction for both students and faculty, which speaks to the motivation of wanting to be preventative rather than reactive.

Will there be more school shootings? Absolutely!

Can we prevent them? Absolutely!

Can we get mentally ill children and youth the help they need in schools? Absolutely!

Can we train educators to be better aware of the warning signs for troubled students? Absolutely!

Can we all be safe in our schools and communities again? Absolutely!

I would like to end this book on a positive note of hope. I believe that human beings are generally good and that most individuals will not resort to this kind of violence. We need to make sure that all individuals within any society feel that they are valued and accepted and have a sense of belonging to someone or something.

Only by making sure that all individuals have a right to freedom, safety, and respect can we ensure that school shootings will be something from our past, and know we made the changes needed to enable all individuals to discover where they fit and what they have to contribute to make the world a better place one day at a time.

I wish you a life of harmony and peace.

References

American Psychological Association. 2004. Warning signs of youth violence. www.apahelpcenter.org/featuredtopics/feature.php?id =38, accessed July 29, 2008.

Anderson M. A., J. Kaufman, T. R. Simon, L. Barrios, L. Paulozzi, and G. Ryan, et al. 2001. School-associated violent deaths in the United States, 1994–1999. *Journal of the American Medical Association* 286:2695–702.

Astor, R. A., A. Meyers, R. Benbenishty, and M. Rosemond. 2005. School safety interventions: Best practices and programs. *Children and Schools* 27:1.

Author, J. R. 2007. Student kills 8 and himself at Finnish high school. *New York Times*, November 8, A-20.

Bearak, B. 2007. As war enters classrooms, fear grips Afghans. *New York Times*, July 10, A-1.

Beauvais, F., E. Chavez, E. Oetting, J. Deffenbacher, and G. Cornell. 1996. Drug use, violence, and victimization among white American, Mexican American, and American Indian dropouts, students with academic problems, and students in good academic standing. *Journal of Counseling Psychology* 43:292–99

Broder, M. J. 2007. 32 shot dead in Virginia: Worst U.S. gun rampage. *New York Times*, April 17.

Bullying. n.d. Wikipedia.org. www.en.wikipedia.org/wiki/bullying, accessed February 8, 2008.

Centers for Disease Control and Prevention. 2003. Coping with a traumatic event. www.bt.cdc.gov/masscasualties/copingpub.asp, accessed March 3, 2008.

Centers for Disease Control and Prevention. 2006a. Youth risk behavioral surveillance—United States, 2005. MMWR Surveillance Summaries 55(SS-5).

Centers for Disease Control and Prevention 2006b. Youth risk behavioral surveillance—United States, 2005. MMWR 55 (SS-5). www.cdc.gov/ncipc/wisqars/default.htm.

Centers for Disease Control and Prevention. 2007. Web-based injury statistics query and reporting system (WISQARS) [Online]. National Center for Injury Prevention and Control. www.cdc.gov/ncipc/wisqars/default.htm, accessed July 9, 2007.

Center for Disease Control and Prevention. 2008. Youth violence prevention. National Center for Injury Prevention and Control. www.cdc.gov/ncipc/dvp/YVP/school_violence.htm, accessed July 29, 2008.

Centers for Disease Control and Prevention. n.d. Web-based injury statistics query and reporting system (WISQARS). National Center for Injury Prevention and Control. www.cdc.gov/ncipc/wisqars, accessed April 6, 2006.

Center for Professional Development Services. 2007. *Bullying prevention*. Bloomington, Ind.: Phi Delta Kappa International. www.pdkintl.org/publications/classtips.htm.

Cornell, D. G., et al. 2004. Guidelines for student threat assessment: Field-test findings. *School Psychology Review* 33:527–46.

Crick, N. R., and M. A. Bigbee. 1998. Relational and overt forms of peer victimization: A multi-informant approach. *Journal of Consulting and Clinical Psychology* 66:337–47.

Crick, N. R., and J. K. Grotpeter. 1996. Children's treatment by peers: Victims of relational and overt aggression. *Development and Psychopathology* 8:367–80.

Donna, M., S. Antonio, and A. E. Salzfass. 2007. How we treat one another in school. *Educational Leadership* 64 (8): 32–38.

FBI. 2007. *Crime in the United States, 2005*. Washington, D.C.: U.S. Department of Justice. www.fbi.gov/ucr/05cius, accessed July 9, 2008.

Federal Bureau of Investigation (FBI). Four-Prong Assessment. www.fbi.gov/publications/school/school2.pdf (accessed April 20, 2007).

Hawkins, J. D., D. Lishner, and R. F. Catalano. 1995. Childhood predictors and the prevention of adolescent substance abuse. In *NIDA Research Monograph No. 56, The Etiology of Drug Abuse: Implications for Prevention*, 75–126. Rockville, Md.: National Institute on Drug Abuse.

Henry, S. 2000. What is school violence? An integrated definition. *Annals of The American Academy of Political and Social Science* 567:16–29.

Indianapolis Star. 2006. Timelines of incidents: School violence around the world. www.indystar.com, accessed April 14, 2008.

Kauffman, P., X. Chen, S. Choy, et al. 2000. Indicators of school crime and safety, 2000 (NCES 2001-017/NCJ-184176). Washington, D.C.: U.S. Department of Education and U.S. Department of Justice.

Kerr, M. 2008. *School crisis prevention and intervention*. Pearson, N.J.

Kerr, M. M., D. A. Brent, B. McKain, and P. S. McCommons. 2006. *Postvention standards manual: A guide for a school's response in the aftermath of a sudden death*. 5th ed. Pittsburgh, Pa.: Services for Teens at Risk, University of Pittsburgh.

Kowalski, R., et al. 2005. Electronic bullying among school-aged children and youth. Poster presented at the annual meeting of the American Psychological Association. Washington, D.C.

McCarthy, C. 1998. *What are gang characteristics?* Official proceedings of the 1998 second international gang specialist training conference. Vol. 1, p. 443.

Muscott, H. 2006. *Anger cycle*. PBIS Intervention Manual. Manchester, N.H.: Center for Positive Behavior Interventions.

Nansel, T. R., M. D. Overpeck, D. L. Haynie, W. J. Ruan, and P. C. Scheidt. 2003. Relationships between bullying and violence among U.S. youth. *Archives of Pediatric and Adolescent Medicine* 157 (4): 348–53.

Nansel, T. R., M. Overpeck, R. Pilla, W. Ruan, B. Simons-Morton, and P. Scheidt. 2001. Bullying behaviors among U.S. youth: Prevalence and association with psychosocial adjustment. *Journal of the American Medical Association* 285:2094–100.

National Education Association. Crisis information. www.nea.org/index.html, accessed July 29, 2008.

National Mental Health Information Center. n.d. *Tips for talking to children after a disaster*. Substance Abuse and Mental Health

Services Administration. www.mentalhealth.samhsa.gov/cmhs
.katrina/parent_teach.asp, accessed March 3, 2008.

Occupational Safety and Health Administration. 1998. *Recommendations for workplace violence prevention programs in retail establishments*. Washington D.C.: U.S. Department of Labor. www.osha
.gov/Publications/osha3153.html, accessed March 10, 2008.

Office of the State Comptroller. *Reporting of violent and disruptive incidents by public schools*. State Education Report 2005-S-38. www
.osc.state.ny.us, accessed May 22, 2006.

Opinion Research Corporation. 2006. *Cyber bully pre-teen*. Princeton, N.J.: Opinion Research Corporation. www.fightcrime.org/cyber
bullying/cyberbullyingpreteen.pdf, accessed July 29, 2008.

Patchin, J. W., and S. Hinduja. 2006. Bullies move beyond the school-yard: A preliminary look at cyberbullying. *Youth Violence and Juvenile Justice* 4 (2): 148–169.

Phi Delta Kappa. 2007. 5 tips for confronting electronic bullying. *Classroom Tips*. www.pdkintl.org/publications/classtips.htm, accessed March 7, 2008.

Prinstein, M. J., J. Boergers, and E. M. Vernberg. 2001. Overt and relational aggression in adolescents: Social-psychological adjustment of aggressors and victims. *Journal of Clinical Child Psychology* 30:479–91.

Reardon, A. B. 1995. *Educating for human dignity*. Philadelphia: University of Pennsylvania Press.

Ringwalt, C. L., S. Ennett, and R. Johnson. 2003. Factors associated with fidelity to substance use prevention curriculum guides in the nation's middle schools. *Health Education & Behavior* 30:375–91.

Saulny, S., and M. Gay. 2008. After shootings Illinois campus prepares to mourn victims. *New York Times*, February 17, A-25.

Sengupta, S. 2007. In India, rare school shooting kills 14 year old. *New York Times*, December 12, A-10.

Sterba, M. and J. Davis. 1999. *Dangerous kids. Boys town approach for helping caregivers treat aggressive and violent youth*. Boys Town, Neb.: Boys Town.

Storch, E. A., M. K. Nock, C. Masia-Warner, and M. E. Barlas. 2003. Peer victimization and social-psychological adjustment in Hispanic and African-American children. *Journal of Child & Family Studies* 12:439–55.

Substance Abuse and Mental Health Services Administration (SAMHSA). 2002. *Communicating in a crisis: Risk communication guidelines for public officials.* Rockville, Md.: U.S. Department of Health and Human Services.

Taylor, J. F. 1991. *Anger control training for children and teens. The adult's guidebook for teaching healthy handling of anger.* Warminster, Pa.: Mar-co Products.

U.S. Department of Education. n.d. Exploring the nature and prevention of bullying. www.ed.gov/admins/lead/safety/training/bullying/index.html, accessed February 4, 2008.

U.S. Department of Education, Office of Safe and Drug Free Schools. 2003. *Practical information on crisis planning: A guide for schools and communities.* www.ed.gov/admin/lead/safety/crisisplanning.pdf, accessed March 9, 2008.

U.S Department of Homeland Security. 2003. Health update, homeland security chemical threat information. www.keytosafer schools.com, accessed March 9, 2008.

Walker, H., and E. Ramsey. 2006. *Anti-social behaviors in school age children.* Thomson Wadsworth publishers, USA.

Wei, H., and J. H. Williams. 2004. Relationship between peer victimization and school adjustment in sixth-grade students: Investigating mediation effects. *Violence and Victims* 19:557–71.

Willard, N. 2006. A parent's guide to cyber bullying, Center for Safe and Responsible Internet Used, accessed March 2, 2008. mdepaolo .myweb.usf.edu/index.html.

Wright, J. 2003. Preventing classroom bullying: What teachers can do. www.jimwrightonline.com/pdfdocs/bully/bullyBooklet.pdf, accessed February 23, 2008.

Wolak, J., K. Mitchell, and D. Finkelhor. 2006. Online victimization of youth: Five years later. Alexandria, Va.: National Center for Missing & Exploited Children.

Yablonsky, L. 1997. *Gangsters: Fifty years of madness, drugs, and death on the streets of America.* New York: New York University Press.

Ybarra, M. L., and K. J. Mitchell. 2004. Youth engaging in online harassment: Associations with caregiver-child relationships, Internet use, and personal characteristics. *Journal of Adolescence* 27:319–36.

About the Author

Dr. Marcel Lebrun has been an educator for twenty-nine years. During that time he has been a classroom teacher, administrator, school counselor, and special education teacher. He was the director of a stress and anxiety clinic from 1994–2002 and a university counselor from 2002–2005. He is presently a professor at Plymouth State University in the Department of Education. He teaches classes in special education, behavior management, counseling, and educational methodology at the undergraduate and graduate level. He has taught abroad and traveled extensively throughout the world. Lebrun has published several books on depression, sexual orientation, and academic strategies, and is presently working on two new books, one on juvenile psychopaths and the other on the dangers in schools and cyberspace. He has published several articles on behavior issues and mental health concerns in children. He is presently on the leadership team for the Positive Behavior Intervention and Supports initiative in New Hampshire. He also provides consulting services to several school districts in need of improvement. Lebrun works mostly with school personnel around student issues in violence, aggression, functional assessment, and mental health concerns. He has presented throughout the United States, Canada, and Asia.

Dr. Lebrun was recently honored with Distinguished Professor of the Year for 2008.